THE EDUCATION ESTABLISHMENT

THE AMERICAN ESTABLISHMENTS SERIES

EDWIN M. SCHUR, *general editor*

Each book in the AMERICAN ESTABLISHMENTS series examines a single, broadly defined "vested interest" in our society. The volumes focus on power and resistance to change in these American institutions, providing a radical reassessment of their future influence.

Elizabeth L. Useem is Assistant Professor of Sociology at Boston State College. Michael Useem is Assistant Professor of Sociology at Harvard University.

THE EDUCATION ESTABLISHMENT

edited by ELIZABETH L. AND MICHAEL USEEM

A SPECTRUM BOOK

PRENTICE-HALL, INC., *Englewood Cliffs, New Jersey*

Library of Congress Cataloging in Publication Data

USEEM, ELIZABETH L   comp.
    The education establishment.

    (American establishments series) (A Spectrum Book)
    Includes bibliographies.
    1. School management and organization—United States.
I. Useem, Michael, joint comp. II. Title.
LB2805.U83 1974   379'.15'0973   74–1250
ISBN 0–13–236562–6
ISBN 0–13–236554–5 (pbk.)

Printed in the United States of America

PRENTICE-HALL INTERNATIONAL, INC. (*London*)
PRENTICE-HALL OF AUSTRALIA PTY. LTD. (*Sydney*)
PRENTICE-HALL OF CANADA, LTD. (*Toronto*)
PRENTICE-HALL OF INDIA PRIVATE LIMITED (*New Delhi*)
PRENTICE-HALL OF JAPAN, INC. (*Tokyo*)

Contents

vii

THE EDUCATION ESTABLISHMENT

Introduction

ELIZABETH L. USEEM AND
MICHAEL USEEM

The great political upheavals of the last decade in America
—civil rights struggles, student rebellions, antiwar protests, inner-
city revolts, prison uprisings—have left one common legacy. This
is a better understanding of American politics and major national
institutions, including education. Assaults on official authority and
the status quo by these political movements have revealed what
normal politics usually obscures: that the present social order is
dominated by entrenched elites. Social movements have also helped
show that the true character of these elites is more profound—and
more obscure—than the identities of its most prominent representatives. The institutional forces sustaining an establishment are most
evident when the establishment must function under political du-
ress.

Fortunately, recent political challenges have been accompanied
by a revival of scholarly interest in society's elites and their social
bases. The resurgence of critical social science, the growth of inves-
tigative journalism, and the spread of independent radical research
organizations have brought an outpouring of material on America's
establishments. Together with traditional academic studies and data
gathered from political conflicts, critical inquiries have led to significant advances in the description and analysis of U.S. elites (for
a sampling of research, see Miliband, 1969; Domhoff, 1967, 1970;
and Prewitt and Stone, 1973). This volume focuses on the establishment in education.

As with any institution, a key question in studying education is
this: Who runs the system? Which organizations, associations, and
pivotal positions influence both the day-to-day operation of schools
and their long-range development? Another important question is
how these established groups came to assume a dominant role in
determining education policy. One way to approach both questions

1

is to look at the social organization of the school system and the role of groups within it, such as students, teachers, and administrators. Yet such a focus is clearly too limited, for education is not an autonomous system. Other institutions have a stake in how schools prepare American youth for entry into adulthood, particularly for occupational roles. Consequently, much of the content and structure of the educational process reflects not only internal pressures but outside constraints as well. This raises still other questions: What are the functions of education in the United States? What is the structure of power in American society? Thus, analysis of the education establishment requires consideration of the political context of schooling in American life.

THE HIDDEN ESTABLISHMENT

To understand the origins of major social patterns in education, it is not enough to refer only to the decisions of policy-makers either within or without the educational system. One must also examine less visible institutional forces, as Samuel Bowles and Jerome Karabel have done in demonstrating how such forces create a highly stratified educational structure. Their selections in this volume reveal that more privileged students are apt to attend better endowed schools, to progress through successive educational levels, and to face better job prospects afterwards. This stratification is partly a consequence of decisions by governing bodies, but it is also the result of more subtle and unintended social forces. This "hidden establishment" is, in fact, often more imporant in setting the fundamental patterns of education than the organized establishment. Consequently, attention must be directed to both the formal power groupings and the less visible institutional and social class pressures.

As Bowles and other analysts argue, formal education performs three critical functions in American society. It provides (1) extended technical training needed for many occupations, (2) an opportunity to mold the new generation's personalities and values, and (3) a comprehensive mechanism for channeling the nation's youth into a finely graded occupational system (see Parsons, 1959; Gintis, 1970; and Collins, 1971). These functions are determined by the economy, social class structure, and general character of American life. For example, special training programs in computer technology and data processing have been introduced in community colleges as the market for programmers has expanded. While it is clear that education has come to serve industry in this fashion, the evolution and sustenance of this relationship are less obvious.

Industry and its representatives have made repeated efforts to directly influence educational decisions. During the period of rapid growth in public schooling in the late nineteenth and early twentieth centuries, business associations and leaders worked to fit the expanding educational system into the emerging industrial order. Because a steady flow of trained, disciplined, and culturally assimilated workers was essential to the social organization of mass production, businessmen and their allies among educational administrators urged appropriate school reforms. Vocational programs and educational testing to rank students were emphasized; business methods were applied to managing schools; and a school's success was measured by the occupational fortunes of its students. The new thrust was apparent in a 1909 description by the Boston School Committee of a school for working-class children: "Everything must conform as closely as possible to actual industrial work in real life. . . . The method must be practical, and both product and method must be subjected to the same commercial tests, as far as possible, as apply to actual industry." (Quoted in Cohen and Lazerson, 1971; also see Curti, 1959; Callahan, 1962; Katz, 1968, 1971; Lazerson, 1971; Greer, 1972; and Spring, 1972.)

The preponderance of business representatives on public school boards and college boards of trustees has provided industry with one direct channel for shaping educational policies in accord with its manpower requirements. Yet a number of less overt links also help transmit capitalist demands to the educational system. This means that in many instances corporate executives need not personally intervene in school affairs to ensure that graduates will harmoniously enter adult work roles. This also implies that certain strategies for change—such as replacing current educational leadership with anti-capitalist members—have their limits.

The economy and its associated social class structure indirectly shape the goals and organization of schools in various ways. For example, it is widely known that schools provide the credentials necessary for climbing the occupational ladder. Local communities pressure school officials to offer programs that raise student achievement scores. Prospective college students strive for entry into the "best" colleges, since a prestigious degree is correctly perceived as a ticket to economic ascent. Thus, administrators are compelled to enhance the occupational chances of their students by bringing the schools into closer compliance with the occupational marketplace. The business elite does not have to encourage such steps—they are a natural consequence of the use of educational credentials to limit entry into the nation's most desirable jobs.

Another informal link between education and the economy is the impact of class background on a student's prospects for educational advancement. Standardized achievement tests used for assigning pupils to ability-level groups and for admissions to colleges and universities give children from wealthy families a competitive advantage over those from poor and working-class backgrounds. In addition, overt discrimination in school assignment and admissions policies hurts marginal ethnic groups. On the whole, poorer students, whatever their academic abilities, are more likely to leave school than their richer classmates. Also, the methods used to finance education in America bestow greater educational resources upon the affluent, and although there are exceptions to these patterns (e.g., some scholarship programs are limited to needy students), school policies repeatedly tend to favor the privileged. It should be noted, however, that such patterns are usually not primarily the result of conscious efforts by elite decision-makers to design a system that discriminates against poor and working-class students. For example, early in the twentieth century many administrators were attracted to standardized testing systems such as that of the College Entrance Examination Board because they made college admissions procedures more orderly. Equal access to college was not a paramount concern at the time, and it proved to be one casualty of the new system (see Schudson, 1972).

Still another instance of the indirect influence of the social order on education is the school's role in instilling values and personality traits required for adult success. As Ralph Miliband and Harmon Zeigler and Wayne Peak have concluded in this volume, school curricula have a conservative cast. Patriotism, capitalism, and the American way of life are celebrated topics, while class and racial conflicts, alternative modes of economic organization, and social problems are either ignored or raised only for critical discussion and ultimate rejection. Zeigler and Peak's analysis documents the conservative bias of public school curricula, such as the chauvinist view of the American economic order contained in one widely used textbook: "We believe that a well regulated capitalism—a free choice, individual incentives, private enterprise system—is the best guarantee of the better life for all mankind." Traditional classroom structures also inculcate personality traits such as punctuality and submissiveness to authority—attributes which make for effective employees (see Litt, 1963, and Gintis, 1971). Teachers encourage these values partly because school systems experience explicit pressures to maintain a conservative curriculum and strict control over their students. However, as Zeigler and Peak argue, teachers are also conventional because they have been trained in relatively traditional and authoritarian schools of education. And while teacher training programs may not be consciously designed to produce teachers loyal to the status quo, this nonetheless is a major outcome. Thus the American educational system is deeply influenced by the American economic order and social class structure. Business interests have an impact in areas far removed from the immediate concerns of production and sale of goods.

THE PUBLIC SCHOOL
ESTABLISHMENT

Civics textbooks often suggest that the public exercises democratic control over the community school through election of the school board. But available research leads to the contrary conclusion that the citizenry has little to do with the formulation of school policies. Voter turnout in school board elections is low and attendance at school board meetings is sparse (two-thirds of the nation's boards usually have fewer than five visitors at their meetings). When the public is mobilized, it is usually for a negative purpose, such as the rejection of a school bond issue at the polls or a fight against controversial curricula or racial desegregation (for a case study of the latter, see Rubin, 1972). Few positive programs result from direct public pressure (see Martin, 1962; Gittell, 1967; Iannaccone, 1967; and Koerner, 1968).

In the absence of public accountability, the sector most likely to have a major voice in school policies is the local economic elite. Studies of decision-making at the community level have found that business leaders are centrally involved in a full spectrum of decisions affecting the public welfare (see Hawley and Wirt, 1968; Aiken and Mott, 1970; and Perrucci and Pilisuk, 1970). Education is no exception.

In the United States, legal authority to administer the schools is vested in the states, which in turn have delegated much of their authority to thousands of local school districts. The formal governing bodies on the local level are the school boards, and dozens of investigations have consistently revealed that local economic elites are disproportionately represented on these bodies. For instance, one review of the research—discussed in the selection by Mario Fantini, Marilyn Gittell, and Richard Magat—concludes that businessmen and professionals comprise more than three-fifths of school board members, while blue-collar workers account for only one-tenth. The article in this volume by W. W. Charters questions whether it is legitimate to infer from such findings that schools are controlled by the local upper class in a fashion which favors their own class interests over other class interests. He argues that it remains to be demonstrated empirically that board members are guided by occupational and class loyalties in setting school policies. And even if this is the case, he maintains it is not clear that the decisions are necessarily contrary to the welfare of other classes underrepresented on school boards.

Indeed, researchers have found that in some cases school board members who are identified with the middle or upper class hold more liberal and progressive views on education than those drawn from the working class (Arnett, 1932; Gross, 1958; Carver, 1968; Rubin, 1972). Moreover, Fantini, Gittell, and Magat maintain that actual control over school operation often resides not in the board but in the school administration—whose bureaucrats are generally not members of the local elite. But it is clear that whenever divergent class perspectives exist on educational programs, as they often do, the local economic elite is in a strategic position to advance its special concerns.

Whatever the extent of formal business influence on the public schools, case studies of power at the community level have shown that business notables frequently influence school policies in an informal way, particularly in small towns. Behind the scenes, pressures are placed on school officials, crucial decisions are covertly made before school board meetings are held, and some issues are simply eliminated from active consideration (Hunter, 1953; Goldhammer, 1955; Vidich and Bensman, 1958; Kimbrough, 1964; Crain and Vanecko, 1968). However, business control is far from absolute. It is constrained by the pressures of a variety of groups and organizations centrally concerned with the educational process. Nothing approximating a coherent, conscious elite controls public education, yet the organizations, groups, and positions most involved in setting educational priorities are generally not accountable to students, parents, or the community at large.

One of the most powerful local groups in the public school establishment consists of professional educators—school administrators and teachers. The power of tenured bureaucrats and instructors to preserve the status quo and undermine reform has been widely observed, although their capacity to do so varies from system to system (Rogers, 1968; Gittell, 1967; Martin, 1962). Other crucial groups at the local level include the school board, teachers' associations such as the National Education Association and the American Federation of Teachers (see the Brenton selection in this volume), and community political officials, particularly the mayors of certain cities. The relative influence of these "core participants" varies by locale and by issue. Rosenthal's (1969b) study of educational governance in five large cities found that the mayors in Boston and New York had a major impact on salary and budgetary matters. In Atlanta the school board and superintendent jointly exercised the dominant voice in financial affairs. In Chicago the superintendent stood out, while in San Francisco the school board had primary control. With the exception of the United Federation of Teachers in New York City, this study found that teachers' associations generally did not exert crucial influence on salary decisions, though this is a primary teacher concern. On personnel and curriculum decisions, the superintendent and his staff were generally the major wielders of influence in all locales. Decisions on the organization of the school system rested primarily with the school superintendent although this power was shared to some extent with the school board.

The governance of education is a state function, and states constrain their school boards by regulating many areas, from textbooks to teacher certification. However, as Frederick Wirt and Michael Kirst indicate in their selection, considerable variation exists among the states in the latitude allowed local school boards. Major participants in school politics at the state level include the governor and legislature, state board of education, and department of education. Various interest groups are also active—statewide teachers' and administrators' associations, state affiliates of the National School Boards Association, and, at times, religious groups, the state Parent-Teachers Association, taxpayers organizations, and certain business interests. On one major state level issue—state financial aid for elementary and secondary schools—Kirst (1970) concludes that no single group, organization, or position has been able to muster a commanding influence. Consequently, political alliances of groups favoring increased school spending have usually formed at a statewide level, although their structures vary from a monolithic coalition in New York to a fragmented and internally divided alliance in Michigan (Iannaccone, 1967).

Federal interest in school affairs has been growing, although its influence is still weak compared with that of state and local governing bodies. Federal court decisions over the past two decades have had a significant impact on school desegregation, school prayer, aid to nonpublic schools, and the legal rights of teachers and students. Federal assistance to public education was dramatically increased in the 1960s, especially with the passage of the Elementary and Secondary Education Act of 1965, but the proportion of school revenues contributed by the national government remains small (7 percent in 1970, up from 4 percent in 1960). The 1960s also saw the rise in size and importance of the U.S. Office of Education, some of whose functions (particularly the funding of research) were acquired by the National Institute of Education upon its creation in 1972.

As at the state level, no single organization or group dominates national educational policy. Major bills to aid elementary and secondary education have passed only through the efforts of key legislative leaders, together with active lobbying by a coalition of interest groups that included the National Education Association and other professional groups, the Parent-Teachers Association, labor unions, civil rights groups, and religious organizations (see Meranto, 1967; Bailey and Mosher, 1968). Administrators in the U.S. Office of Education and other federal agencies set the guidelines for disbursement of Congressional appropriations, and their decisions have an independent bearing on how the money is actually spent (Bailey and Mosher, 1968).

Other organizations and groups influence school policies in more limited areas. These include accreditation agencies that review program quality in secondary schools and colleges, industries that are involved in marketing school related products, testing agencies whose standardized tests for college admissions inevitably shape the curricula of the public schools, private foundations that have thrown their financial support behind experimental educational programs, and schools of education that determine who shall be teachers and how they are trained.

This evidence indicates that direct day-to-day control of elementary and secondary schooling rests in the hands of an elite that is relatively impervious to public influence. This elite is dominated by professional educators and bureaucrats more than by any other group, but its exact composition and the relative strength of the various members depends on local factors. Representatives of the upper class have a disproportionate voice in daily school affairs, but their control is primarily exercised in more subtle and indirect ways.

THE ESTABLISHMENT IN HIGHER EDUCATION

A common misconception about public schools is that they are subject to popular control, and a comparable myth in higher education is that the college faculty is sovereign. Faculties often control important curriculum and hiring decisions, but they have little influence on the institution's overall budget, selection of administrators, long-range planning, and relations with the local community. Moreover, faculty power is a delegated authority. While such authority is difficult to withdraw, campus conflict has shown that administrators and governing boards will often overrule faculty decisions.

Legal authority for the governance of the college is normally invested in a board of trustees. In private institutions new trustees are generally elected by the board itself although religious groups and alumni select new members at some institutions. The preponderant pattern in public colleges is for trustees to be appointed by a state governor or other government official. Public influence in either case is negligible. If boards of trustees are not publicly accountable, the occupational profile of the boards suggests that as in the case of public school boards, they are more responsive to business than other outside interests.

"The discretionary control of matters of university policy now rests finally in the hands of businessmen," wrote Thorstein Veblen early in this century. He was commenting on a new breed of trustees who had displaced a clergyman-majority on many governing boards. Corroborating evidence is offered by McGrath (1936) in his study of trustees at 20 representative institutions from 1860 to 1930. Businessmen, bankers, and lawyers held more than two-thirds of the seats at state institutions throughout this period. At private colleges the business groups steadily gained strength over the seven decades, finally holding three out of four positions in 1930. Rodney Hartnett's 1968 national survey of trustees—an excerpt is included in this volume—disclosed that business executives and attorneys were still by far the largest occupational groups represented. Of the nearly 4,000 trustees at public and non-Catholic private colleges surveyed by Hartnett, approximately half were lawyers or business executives, while less than one in 100 were labor leaders.

Charters' article in this volume asks whether a school board member's social class necessarily affects his decisions on educational matters. The same question can be raised about businessmen on college boards of trustees. Hartnett asked trustees to express their opinions on a number of matters, including whether "running a college is basically like running a business" and whether "experience in high-level business management" was essential for a new college president. He found that trustees who were industry executives were more likely to agree on the need for business experience. Whether this business outlook affects the routine teaching functions of the college is debatable, since it can be argued that curriculum and hiring issues are rarely discussed by governing boards. However, the Hartnett study found that a majority of trustees at all types of institutions claimed to be involved in decisions on faculty appointments, changes in the undergraduate program, and instructional methods. Roughly two-thirds of the trustees maintained that they and/or the college administration should have the *only* say on faculty tenure decisions. More than half agreed it was reasonable to require faculty members to sign a loyalty oath, and two-fifths felt the administration should "control the contents" of the student newspaper. Another study shows that the pressure for firing controversial faculty members has usually come from the college administration and trustees rather than from the local community, state legislature, or faculty. Typically, political views of fired faculty members were the central issue, rather than their teaching or research abilities (Lewis, 1964; Lewis and Ryan, 1971).

Business influence on college policies is also exercised informally. For instance, private colleges depend on financial contributions for economic survival, and the largest private benefactors are likely to be members of the upper class, private foundations whose endowments typically derive from business wealth, and corporations. Predictably, there is a tendency to mute criticism of the private enterprise system, a point underscored in Miliband's selection. Even without overt links, assumptions shared by college and business leaders often produce the same outcome. In analyzing the growth of vocational training programs in community colleges, Karabel concludes that management does not usually intervene when special programs are set up to train workers for technical positions in industry. Rather, as one observer (Cohen, 1971) put it, business philosophy is so widely held by junior college administrators that they "trip over each other in their haste to organize a new technical curriculum" when "corporate managers . . . announce a need for skilled workers."

Because higher education is heavily dependent on public funds, federal and state governments obviously have great leverage in setting educational policies. In 1970, roughly 40 percent of the nation's 2,500 institutions of higher education were public; about 70 percent of the country's seven million college students were enrolled in public institutions. In that year, nearly 58 percent of the public college expenditures came from public revenues, of which state governments contributed nearly two-thirds. Even in private schools, 21 percent of the expenditures came from government sources, especially the federal government. Of the 1970 funds for institutions of higher education, the federal government accounted for 17 percent, the states for 25 percent, and local governments for 4 percent. The *absolute* investment of all three levels of government rose sharply during the 1960s—the federal contribution reached $14 billion in 1970, up from $1 billion ten years earlier—but the *relative* contribution of public financing remained stable over this period. Public revenues constituted 42 percent of the total in 1960 and 45 percent in 1970.

Jencks and Riesman (1968) argue that the source of financing often has greater effect on the character of a college than the composition of its board of trustees. Because of the different methods of financing, tuition at public schools in 1966 was less than a quarter of that charged by private institutions. This disparity in tuition costs, rather than the different types of governing boards is a major reason for the $2,000 gap between the median income of parents of students at public and private institutions. It is also clear that the four-fold increase in federal funds for academic research in the 1960s was chiefly responsible for the vast expansion of the campus research complex during that decade. The government has shown that it will not hesitate to use this financial leverage to spur certain policy changes. One example is the federal government's threats to withhold funds from schools that have continued to discriminate in the hiring of women and minority group members.

Students, staff, faculty, administrators, and trustees all have some political influence on both the internal direction of their own institutions and on public policies affecting higher education. However, student influence on campus—aside from sporadic rebellions—is typically limited to such mundane concerns as dormitory regulations. Student lobbying on significant college-related legislation is practically nonexistent. At many schools faculties have acquired *de facto* control over some major policy areas, especially those related to teaching. However, the major national college teachers' association, the American Association of University Professors (AAUP), has traditionally been a weak group. It has been unable to ensure job security for teachers and has done little to press for faculty power in broader realms. The more militant American Federation of Teachers has attracted increasing numbers of college teachers, and this threat has caused the AAUP to become more assertive. Collective bargaining and teachers' strikes are on the rise at the college level, but the overall influence of the faculty on most major college policies remains small.

The daily operations of colleges and universities is primarily in the hands of presidents and other top administrators. At the same time, these officials form an important national power bloc through administrator-dominated associations. One of the most influential of these is the American Council on Education, which has been described as the "main trade association representing the managers of the higher education industry" (Lauter and Alexander, 1969). Although its membership includes over 1,300 highly diverse colleges and universities, its Board of Directors has been controlled by administrators from the more prestigious schools. Other nationally important administrator groups include the Association of Land Grant Colleges and Universities and the American Association of Junior Colleges. Administrators also control other agencies that shape the goals and structure of higher education, particularly the accrediting agencies and testing organizations.

Groups that are relatively unimportant in the power structure of academe—such as students, the faculty, and the local community— are usually weak only because they lack effective organization. The success of radical student groups in mobilizing large numbers of students against college administration policies during the late 1960s demonstrated the power of organized students. Campus protest changed administration positions on a number of issues, including campus military recruitment, student influence on faculty hiring, and introduction of black studies programs (Bayer and Astin, 1969; Astin and Bayer, 1971; Morgan, 1972).

The campus struggles of this era also revealed that higher education policies serving the interests of government and business create conditions on campus that alienate and mobilize students. The Vietnam–era conscription policy of deferring young men while they attended college and of using class-standing as a criterion for drafting some students created intense competitive pressures among students to remain in school and to achieve high grades. Similarly, the college's role in socializing students for unrewarding jobs leads to similar alienating conditions on campus. Students are encouraged to seek extrinsic rewards in their school work, such as grades, rather than intrinsic satisfactions. Student voice on matters of any significance is negligible, a situation that parallels their future powerlessness once they are employed. Critical thought and action is discouraged, while submissiveness to immediate superiors—the teacher (and later the supervisor)—is reinforced. Grievances stemming from these and other problems have repeatedly appeared in the programs, demands, and general objectives of the student rebellions of the 1960s (see Rowntree and Rowntree, 1968; Gintis, 1970; Bowles, 1972; Flacks, 1971; Miles, 1971; and Friedman, 1973).

Thus, the dominant groups in higher education include top college administrators, governing boards with their heavy business representation, and state and national governments. While students may often regard faculty members as despots, both teachers and students are relatively powerless to affect the major decisions in higher education. It has been primarily through the exercise of collective strength and militant actions, such as teacher strikes and student protests, that these groups have made inroads against the power of the administration and trustees, and the privileged interests they represent.

THE FUTURE OF EDUCATIONAL GOVERNANCE

The relative influence of certain groups in education—particularly that of the federal and state governments, school superintendents, and teachers' organizations—appears to be on the rise. Although students and community groups have sharply increased their demands for representation in school politics, there are few signs that they will win genuine participation in the near future.

Despite the entrenched power of the establishment in public and higher education, schools are probably more vulnerable to change than most other organizations. While schools reflect the needs of society's dominant institutions, they may at the same time serve to undermine the established capitalist order. It is generally easier for critics of American life to express their dissent in the classroom than in an office or on the factory line. The privacy of the classroom and the traditional norms of academic freedom provide considerable latitude for voicing critical views. Also, students are relatively unencumbered by dependents and debts and are therefore more able to take the risks of militant actions against college administrations than they are to take similar actions against employers.

Reformers should not operate under the illusion that schools are the central agency of social change. But school personnel can play an important role in encouraging significant numbers of students and faculty to develop the awareness and political skills needed to attack the primary centers of power and privilege in American society.

REFERENCES

AIKEN, MICHAEL, AND PAUL E. MOTT, editors, *The Structure of Community Power*. New York: Random House, 1970.
ARNETT, CLAUDE E., *Social Beliefs and Attitudes of School Board Members*. Emporia, Kansas: Emporia Gazette Press, 1932.

14   *Elizabeth L. Useem and Michael Useem*

ASTIN, ALEXANDER W., AND ALAN E. BAYER, "Antecedents and Consequents of Disruptive Campus Protest," *Measurement and Evaluation in Guidance*, 4 (April, 1971): 18–30.

BAILEY, STEPHEN K., AND EDITH K. MOSHER, *ESEA: The Office of Education Administers a Law*. Syracuse, N.Y.: Syracuse University Press, 1968.

BAYER, ALAN E., AND ALEXANDER W. ASTIN, "Violence and Disruption on the U.S. Campus, 1968–1969," *Educational Record*, 50 (Fall, 1969): 337–50.

BOWLES, SAMUEL, "Contradictions in Higher Education in the United States," in *The Capitalist System: A Radical Analysis of American Society*, edited by Richard C. Edwards, Michael Reich, and Thomas E. Weisskopf. Englewood Cliffs, N.J.: Prentice-Hall, 1972.

CALLAHAN, RAYMOND, *Education and the Cult of Efficiency*. Chicago: University of Chicago Press, 1962.

CARVER, FRED D., "Social Class and School Board Role Expectations," *Urban Education*, 3 (1968): 153–54.

COHEN, ARTHUR M., "Stretching Pre-College Education," *Social Policy*, 2 (May/June, 1971): 5–9.

COHEN, DAVID, AND MARVIN LAZERSON, "Education and the Corporate Order," *Socialist Revolution*, 8 (March–April, 1972): 47–72.

COLLINS, RANDALL, "Functional and Conflict Theories of Educational Stratification," *American Sociological Review*, 36 (December, 1971): 1002–19.

CRAIN, ROBERT L., *The Politics of School Desegregation*. Chicago: Aldine Publishing Company, 1968.

CRAIN, ROBERT L., AND JAMES J. VANECKO, "Elite Influence in School Desegregation," in *City Politics and Public Policy*, edited by James Q. Wilson. New York: John Wiley & Sons, 1968.

CURTI, MERLE, *The Social Ideas of American Educators*. Totowa, N.J.: Littlefield, Adams & Co., 1959 (originally published in 1935).

DOMHOFF, G. WILLIAM, *Who Rules America?* Englewood Cliffs, N.J.: Prentice-Hall, 1967.

———, *The Higher Circles*. New York: Random House, 1970.

FLACKS, RICHARD, *Youth and Social Change*. Chicago: Markham Publishing Company, 1971.

FRIEDMAN, SAMUEL R., "Perspectives on the American Student Movement," *Social Problems*, 20 (Winter, 1973): 283–99.

GINTIS, HERBERT, "New Working Class and Revolutionary Youth," *Socialist Revolution*, 1 (May/June, 1970): 13–43.

———, "Education and the Characteristics of Worker Productivity," *American Economic Review*, 61 (May, 1971): 266–79.

GITTELL, MARILYN, *Participants and Participation: A Study of School Policy in New York City*. New York: Praeger Publishers, 1967.

GITTELL, MARILYN, T. EDWARD HOLLANDER, AND WILLIAM S. VINCENT, "Fiscal Status and School Policy Making in Six Large School Districts," in *The Politics of Education at the Local, State and Federal Levels*, edited by Michael Kirst. Berkeley, California: McCutchan Publishing Corporation, 1970.

GOLDHAMMER, KEITH, "Community Power Structure and School Board Membership," *American School Board Journal,* 130 (1955): 23–25.

GREER, COLIN, *The Great School Legend: A Revisionist Interpretation of American Education.* New York: Basic Books, 1972.

GROSS, NEAL, *Who Runs Our Schools?* New York: John Wiley & Sons, 1958.

HAWLEY, WILLIS D., AND FREDERICK M. WIRT, editors, *The Search for Community Power.* Englewood Cliffs, N.J.: Prentice-Hall, 1968.

HUNTER, FLOYD, *Community Power Structure: A Study of Decision Makers.* Chapel Hill, N.C.: University of North Carolina Press, 1953.

IANNACCONE, LAURENCE, *Politics in Education.* New York: Center for Applied Research in Education, 1967.

JENCKS, CHRISTOPHER, AND DAVID RIESMAN, *The Academic Revolution.* Garden City, N.Y.: Doubleday & Company, 1968.

KATZ, MICHAEL, *The Irony of Early School Reform: Educational Innovation in Mid-Nineteenth Century Massachusetts.* Cambridge, Mass.: Harvard University Press, 1968.

———, *Class, Bureaucracy, and Schools: The Illusion of Educational Change in America.* New York: Praeger Publishers, 1971.

KIMBROUGH, RALPH B., *Political Power and Educational Decision-Making.* Chicago: Rand McNally, 1964.

KIRST, MICHAEL W., editor, *The Politics of Education at the Local, State and Federal Levels.* Berkeley, California: McCutchan Publishing Corporation, 1970.

KOERNER, JAMES D., *Who Controls American Education?* Boston: Beacon Press, 1968.

LAUTER, PAUL, AND ARCHIBALD W. ALEXANDER, "ACE: Defender of the Educational Faith," *The Antioch Review,* 29 (Fall, 1969): 287–303.

LAZERSON, MARVIN, *Origins of the Urban School: Public Education in Massachusetts, 1870–1915.* Cambridge, Mass.: Harvard University Press, 1971.

LEWIS, LIONEL S., "The Academic Axe: Some Trends in Dismissals from Institutions of Higher Learning in America," *Social Problems,* 12 (Fall, 1964): 151–58.

LEWIS, LIONEL S., AND MICHAEL N. RYAN, "In the Matter of University Governance During the 1960's," *Social Problems,* 19 (Fall, 1971): 249–57.

LITT, EDGAR, "Civic Education, Community Norms, and Political Indoctrination," *American Sociological Review,* 29 (February, 1963): 69–75.

MARTIN, ROSCOE, *Government and the Suburban School.* Syracuse, N.Y.: Syracuse University Press, 1962.

McGRATH, EARL J., "The Control of Higher Education in America," *Educational Record,* 17 (April, 1936): 259–72.

MERANTO, PHILIP, *The Politics of Federal Aid to Education in 1965: A Study in Political Innovation.* Syracuse, N.Y.: Syracuse University Press, 1967.

MILES, MICHAEL W., *The Radical Probe: The Logic of Student Rebellion.* New York: Atheneum, 1971.

MILIBAND, RALPH, *The State in Capitalist Society.* New York: Basic Books, 1969.

MORGAN, WILLIAM R., "Campus Conflict as Formative Influence," in *Col-*

lective Violence, edited by James F. Short, Jr. and Marvin E. Wolfgang. Chicago: Aldine-Atherton, 1972.

PARSONS, TALCOTT, "The School Class as a Social System: Some of its Functions in American Society," *Harvard Educational Review,* 29 (Fall, 1959): 297–318.

PERRUCCI, ROBERT, AND MARC PILISUK, "Leaders and Ruling Elites: The Interorganizational Bases of Community Power," *American Sociological Review,* 35 (December, 1970): 1040–57.

PREWITT, KENNETH, AND ALAN STONE, *The Ruling Elites: Elite Theory, Power, and American Democracy.* New York: Harper & Row, 1973.

ROGERS, DAVID, *110 Livingston Street: Politics and Bureaucracy in the New York City School System.* New York: Random House, 1968.

ROSENTHAL, ALAN, editor, *Governing Education: A Reader on Politics, Power, and Public School Policy.* Garden City, N.Y.: Doubleday & Company, 1969a.

———, *Pedagogues and Power: Teacher Groups in School Politics.* Syracuse, N.Y.: Syracuse University Press, 1969b.

ROWNTREE, JOHN, AND MARGARET ROWNTREE, "Youth as a Class," *International Socialist Journal,* 25 (February, 1968): 25–58.

RUBIN, LILLIAN B., *Busing and Backlash: White against White in an Urban School District.* Berkeley, California: University of California Press, 1972.

SCHUDSON, MICHAEL S., "Organizing the 'Meritocracy': A History of the College Entrance Examination Board," *Harvard Educational Review,* 42 (February, 1972): 34–69.

SPRING, JOEL H., *Education and the Rise of the Corporate State.* Boston: Beacon Press, 1972.

VEBLEN, THORSTEIN, *The Higher Learning in America: A Memorandum on the Conduct of Universities by Business Men.* New York: Hill and Wang, 1957 (originally published in 1918).

VIDICH, ARTHUR J., AND JOSEPH BENSMAN, *Small Town in Mass Society.* Princeton, N.J.: Princeton University Press, 1958.

c h a p t e r   o n e

Unequal education
and the reproduction
of the social division of labor

SAMUEL BOWLES

The ideological defense of modern capitalist society rests heavily on the assertion that the equalizing effects of education can counter the disequalizing forces inherent in the free-market system. That educational systems in capitalist societies have been highly unequal is generally admitted and widely condemned. Yet educational inequalities are taken as passing phenomena, holdovers from an earlier, less enlightened era, which are rapidly being eliminated.

The record of educational history in the United States, and scrutiny of the present state of our colleges and schools, lend little support to this comforting optimism. Rather, the available data suggest an alternative interpretation. In what follows I argue (1) that schools have evolved in the United States not as part of a pursuit of equality, but rather to meet the needs of capitalist employers for a disciplined and skilled labor force, and to provide a mechanism for social control in the interests of political stability; (2) that as the economic importance of skilled and well-educated labor has grown, inequalities in the school system have become increasingly important in reproducing the class structure from one generation to the next; (3) that the U.S. school system is pervaded by class inequalities, which have shown little sign of diminishing over the last half cen-

"Unequal Education and the Reproduction of the Social Division of Labor" by Samuel Bowles. From *Review of Radical Political Economics*, vol. 3 (Fall/Winter, 1971). Copyright © 1971 by Samuel Bowles. Reprinted by permission of the author.

Many of the ideas in this essay have been worked out jointly with Herbert Gintis and other members of the Harvard seminar of the Union for Radical Political Economics. I am grateful to them and to Janice Weiss and Christopher Jencks for their help.

tury; and (4) that the evidently unequal control over school boards
and other decision-making bodies in education does not provide a
sufficient explanation of the persistence and pervasiveness of inequalities in the school system. Although the unequal distribution
of political power serves to maintain inequalities in education, the
origins of these inequalities are to be found outside the political
sphere, in the class structure itself and in the class subcultures typical of capitalist societies. Thus, unequal education has its roots in
the very class structure which it serves to legitimize and reproduce.
Inequalities in education are part of the web of capitalist society,
and are likely to persist as long as capitalism survives.

THE EVOLUTION OF CAPITALISM
AND THE RISE OF MASS
EDUCATION

In colonial America, and in most pre-capitalist societies of the
past, the basic productive unit was the family. For the vast majority
of male adults, work was self-directed, and was performed without
direct supervision. Though constrained by poverty, ill health, the
low level of technological development, and occasional interfer-
ences by the political authorities, a man had considerable leeway
in choosing his working hours, what to produce, and how to produce it. While great inequalities in wealth, political power, and
other aspects of status normally existed, differences in the degree of
autonomy in work were relatively minor, particularly when compared with what was to come.

Transmitting the necessary productive skills to the children as
they grew up proved to be a simple task, not because the work was
devoid of skill, but because the quite substantial skills required
were virtually unchanging from generation to generation, and because the transition to the world of work did not require that the
child adapt to a wholly new set of social relationships. The child
learned the concrete skills and adapted to the social relations of
production through learning by doing within the family. Preparation for life in the larger community was facilitated by the child's
experience with the extended family, which shaded off without distinct boundaries, through uncles and fourth cousins, into the community. Children learned early how to deal with complex relationships among adults other than their parents, and children other
than their brothers and sisters.[1]

---

[1] This account draws upon two important historical studies: P. Aries, *Centuries
of Childhood* (New York: Vintage, 1965); and B. Bailyn, *Education in the Forming of American Society* (Chapel Hill: University of North Carolina Press, 1960).

Children were not required to learn a complex set of political principles or ideologies, as political participation was limited and political authority unchallenged, at least in normal times. The only major socializing institution outside the family was the church, which sought to inculcate the accepted spiritual values and attitudes. In addition, a small number of children learned craft skills outside the family, as apprentices. The role of schools tended to be narrowly vocational, restricted to preparation of children for a career in the church or the still inconsequential state bureaucracy.[2] The curriculum of the few universities reflected the aristocratic penchant for conspicuous intellectual consumption.[3]

The extension of capitalist production, and particularly the factory system, undermined the role of the family as the major unit of both socialization and production. Small peasant farmers were driven off the land or competed out of business. Cottage industry was destroyed. Ownership of the means of production became heavily concentrated in the hands of landlords and capitalists. Workers relinquished control over their labor in return for wages or salaries. Increasingly, production was carried on in large organizations in which a small management group directed the work activities of the entire labor force. The social relations of production—the authority structure, the prescribed types of behavior and response characteristic of the work place—became increasingly distinct from those of the family.

The divorce of the worker from control over production—from control over his own labor—is particularly important in understanding the role of schooling in capitalist societies. The resulting social division of labor—between controllers and controlled—is a crucial aspect of the class structure of capitalist societies, and will be seen to be an important barrier to the achievement of social-class equality in schooling.

Also illuminating are anthropological studies of education in contemporary precapitalist societies. See, for example, J. Kenyatta, *Facing Mount Kenya* (New York: Vintage, 1962), pp. 95–124. See also Edmund S. Morgan, *The Puritan Family: Religion and Domestic Relations in Seventeenth Century New England* (New York: Harper and Row, 1966).

[2] Aries, *Centuries of Childhood.* In a number of places, e.g., Scotland and Massachusetts, schools stressed literacy so as to make the Bible more widely accessible. See C. Cipolla, *Literacy and Economic Development* (Baltimore: Penguin Books, 1969); and Morgan, *Puritan Family,* chap. 4. Morgan quotes a Massachusetts law of 1647 which provided for the establishment of reading schools because it was "one chief project of that old deluder, Satan, to keep men from knowledge of the Scriptures."

[3] H. F. Kearney, *Scholars and Gentlemen: Universities and Society in Pre-Industrial Britain* (Ithaca, N.Y.: Cornell University Press, 1971).

Rapid economic change in the capitalist period led to frequent shifts of the occupational distribution of the labor force, and constant changes in the skill requirements for jobs. The productive skills of the father were no longer adequate for the needs of the son during his lifetime. Skill training within the family became increasingly inappropriate.

And the family itself was changing. Increased geographic mobility of labor and the necessity for children to work outside the family spelled the demise of the extended family and greatly weakened even the nuclear family.[4] Meanwhile, the authority of the church was questioned by the spread of secular rationalist thinking and the rise of powerful competing groups.

While undermining the main institutions of socialization, the development of the capitalist system created at the same time an environment—both social and intellectual—which would ultimately challenge the political order. Workers were thrown togther in oppressive factories, and the isolation which had helped to maintain quiescence in earlier, widely dispersed peasant populations was broken down.[5] With an increasing number of families uprooted from the land, the workers' search for a living resulted in large-scale labor migrations. Transient, even foreign, elements came to constitute a major segment of the population, and began to pose seemingly insurmountable problems of assimilation, integration, and control.[6] Inequalities of wealth became more apparent, and were less easily justified and less readily accepted. The simple legitimizing ideologies of the earlier period—the divine right of kings and the divine origin of social rank, for example—fell under the capitalist attack on the royalty and the traditional landed interests. The general broadening of the electorate—first sought by the capitalist class in the struggle against the entrenched interests of the pre-capitalist period—threatened soon to become an instrument for the growing power of the working class. Having risen to political power, the capitalist class sought a mechanism to ensure social control and political stability.[7]

[4] See Bailyn, *Education in the Forming of American Society;* N. Smelser, *Social Change in the Industrial Revolution* (Chicago: University of Chicago Press, 1959).

[5] F. Engels and K. Marx, *The Communist Manifesto* (London, England: G. Allen and Unwin, 1951); K. Marx, *The 18th Brumaire of Louis Bonaparte* (New York: International Publishers, 1935).

[6] See, for example, S. Thernstrom, *Poverty and Progress: Social Mobility in a 19th Century City* (Cambridge: Harvard University Press, 1964).

[7] B. Simon, *Studies in the History of Education, 1780–1870,* vol. 1 (London, England: Lawrence and Wishant, 1960).

An institutional crisis was at hand. The outcome, in virtually all capitalist countries, was the rise of mass education. In the United States, the many advantages of schooling as a socialization process were quickly perceived. The early proponents of the rapid expansion of schooling argued that education could perform many of the socialization functions that earlier had been centered in the family and, to a lesser extent, in the church.[8] An ideal preparation for factory work was found in the social relations of the school: specifically, in its emphasis on discipline, punctuality, acceptance of authority outside the family, and individual accountability for one's work.[9] The social relations of the school would replicate the social relations of the work place, and thus help young people adapt to the social division of labor. Schools would further lead people to accept the authority of the state and its agents—the teachers—at a young age, in part by fostering the illusion of the benevolence of the government in its relations with citizens.[10] Moreover, because schooling would ostensibly be open to all, one's position in the social division of labor could be portrayed as the result not of birth, but of one's

---

[8] Bailyn, *Education in the Forming of American Society*.

[9] A manufacturer, writing to the Massachusetts State Board of Education from Lowell in 1841 commented:

> I have never considered mere knowledge . . . as the only advantage derived from a good Common School education. . . . (Workers with more education possess) a higher and better state of morals, are more orderly and respectful in their deportment, and more ready to comply with the wholesome and necessary regulations of an establishment. . . . In times of agitation, on account of some change in regulations or wages, I have always looked to the most intelligent, best educated and the most moral for support. The ignorant and uneducated I have generally found the most turbulent and troublesome, acting under the impulse of excited passion and jealousy.

Quoted in Michael B. Katz, *The Irony of Early School Reform* (Cambridge, Mass.: Harvard University Press, 1968), p. 88. See also David Isaac Bruck, "The Schools of Lowell, 1824–1861: A Case Study in the Origins of Modern Public Education in America" (Senior thesis, Harvard College, Department of Social Studies, April 1971).

[10] In 1846 the annual report of the Lowell, Mass., School Committee concluded that universal education was "the surest safety against internal commotions" (*1846 School Committee Annual Report*, pp. 17–18). It seems more than coincidental that, in England, public support for elementary education—a concept which had been widely discussed and urged for at least half a century was legislated almost immediately after the enfranchisement of the working class by the electoral reform of 1867. See Simon, *Studies in the History of Education, 1780–1870*. Mass public education in Rhode Island came quickly on the heels of an armed insurrection and a broadening of the franchise. See F. T. Carlton, *Economic Influences upon Educational Progress in the United States, 1820–1850* (New York: Teachers College Press, 1966).

own efforts and talents.[11] And if the children's everyday experiences with the structure of schooling were insufficient to inculcate the correct views and attitudes, the curriculum itself would be made to embody the bourgeois ideology.[12] Where pre-capitalist social institutions, particularly the church, remained strong or threatened the capitalist hegemony, schools sometimes served as a modernizing counter-institution.[13]

The movement for public elementary and secondary education in the United States originated in the nineteenth century in states dominated by the burgeoning industrial capitalist class, most nota-

[11] Describing the expansion of education in the nineteenth century, Katz concludes:

. . . a middle class attempt to secure advantage for their children as technological change heightened the importance of formal education assured the success and acceptance of universal elaborate graded school systems. The same result emerged from the fear of a growing, unschooled proletariat. Education substituted for deference as a source of social cement and social order in a society stratified by class rather than by rank. (M. B. Katz, "From Voluntarism to Bureaucracy in U.S. Education," mimeograph, 1970.)

[12] An American economist, writing just prior to the "common school revival," had this to say:

Education universally extended throughout the community will tend to disabuse the working class of people in respect of a notion that has crept into the minds of our mechanics and is gradually prevailing, that manual labor is at present very inadequately rewarded, owing to combinations of the rich against the poor; that mere mental labor is comparatively worthless; that property or wealth ought not to be accumulated or transmitted; that to take interest on money let or profit on capital employed is unjust. . . . The mistaken and ignorant people who entertain these fallacies as truths will learn, when they have the opportunity of learning, that the institution of political society originated in the protection of property. (Thomas Cooper, *Elements of Political Economy* [1828], quoted in Carlton, *Economic Influences upon Educational Progress in the United States, 1820–1850*, pp. 33–34.)

Political economy was made a required subject in Massachusetts high schools in 1857, along with moral science and civic polity. Cooper's advice was widely but not universally followed elsewhere. Friedrich Engels, commenting on the tardy growth of mass education in early nineteenth-century England, remarked: "So shortsighted, so stupidly narrow-minded is the English bourgeoisie in its egotism, that it does not even take the trouble to impress upon the workers the morality of the day, which the bourgeoisie has patched together in its own interest for its own protection." (Engels, *The Condition of the Working Class in England* [Stanford, Calif.: Stanford University Press, 1968].)

[13] See Thernstrom, *Poverty and Progress*. Marx said this about mid-nineteenth-century France:

The modern and the traditional consciousness of the French peasant contended for mastery . . . in the form of an incessant struggle between the schoolmasters and the priests. (Marx, *The 18th Brumaire of Louis Bonaparte*, p. 125.)

bly in Massachusetts. It spread rapidly to all parts of the country except the South.[14] In Massachusetts the extension of elementary education was in large measure a response to industrialization, and to the need for social control of the Irish and other non-Yankee workers recruited to work in the mills.[15] The fact that some working people's movements had demanded free instruction should not obscure the basically coercive nature of the extension of schooling. In many parts of the country, schools were literally imposed upon the workers.[16]

The evolution of the economy in the nineteenth century gave rise to new socialization needs and continued to spur the growth of education. Agriculture continued to lose ground to manufacturing; simple manufacturing gave way to production involving complex interrelated processes; an increasing fraction of the labor force was employed in producing services rather than goods. Employers in the most rapidly growing sectors of the economy began to require more than obedience and punctuality in their workers; a change in motivational outlook was required. The new structure of production provided little built-in motivation. There were fewer jobs such as farming and piece-rate work in manufacturing in which material reward was tied directly to effort. As work roles became more complicated and interrelated, the evaluation of the individual worker's performance became increasingly difficult. Employers began to look for workers who had internalized the production-related values of the firm's managers.

The continued expansion of education was pressed by many who saw schooling as a means of producing these new forms of motivation and discipline. Others, frightened by the growing labor militancy after the Civil War, found new urgency in the social-control arguments popular among the proponents of education in the antebellum period.

A system of class stratification developed within this rapidly expanding educational system. Children of the social elite normally attended private schools. Because working-class children tended to leave school early, the class composition of the public high schools was distinctly more elite than the public primary schools.[17] And as

[14] Janice Weiss and I are currently studying the rapid expansion of southern elementary and secondary schooling which followed the demise of slavery and the establishment of capitalist economic institutions in the South.

[15] Based on the preliminary results of a statistical analysis of education in nineteenth-century Massachusetts being conducted jointly with Alexander Field.

[16] Katz, *Irony of Early School Reform* and "From Voluntarism to Bureaucracy in U.S. Education."

[17] Katz, *Irony of Early School Reform.*

a university education ceased to be merely training for teaching or the divinity and became important in gaining access to the pinnacles of the business world, upper-class families used their money and influence to get their children into the best universities, often at the expense of the children of less elite families.

Around the turn of the present century, large numbers of working-class and particularly immigrant children began attending high schools. At the same time, a system of class stratification developed within secondary education.[18] The older democratic ideology of the common school—that the same curriculum should be offered to all children—gave way to the "progressive" insistence that education should be tailored to the "needs of the child." [19] In the interests of providing an education relevant to the later life of the students, vocational schools and tracks were developed for the children of working families. The academic curriculum was preserved for those who would later have the opportunity to make use of book learning, either in college or in white-collar employment. This and other educational reforms of the progressive education movement reflected an implicit assumption of the immutability of the class structure.

The frankness with which students were channeled into curriculum tracks, on the basis of their social-class background, raised serious doubts concerning the "openness" of the social-class structure. The relation between social class and a child's chances of promo-

---

[18] Sol Cohen describes this process in "The Industrial Education Movement, 1906–1917," *American Quarterly* 20 no. 1 (Spring 1968): 95–110. Typical of the arguments then given for vocational education is the following, by the superintendent of schools in Cleveland:

> It is obvious that the educational needs of children in a district where the streets are well paved and clean, where the homes are spacious and surrounded by lawns and trees, where the language of the child's playfellows is pure, and where life in general is permeated with the spirit and ideals of America—it is obvious that the educational needs of such a child are radically different from those of the child who lives in a foreign and tenement section. (William H. Elson and Frank P. Bachman, "Different Course for Elementary School," *Educational Review* 39 [April 1910]: 361–63.)

See also L. Cremin, *The Transformation of the School: Progressivism in American Education, 1876–1957* (New York: Alfred A. Knopf, 1961), chap. 2, and David Cohen and Marvin Lazerson, "Education and the Industrial Order," mimeograph, 1970.

[19] The superintendent of the Boston schools summed up the change in 1908:

> Until very recently (the schools) have offered equal opportunity for all to receive *one kind* of education, but what will make them democratic is to provide opportunity for all to receive such education as will fit them *equally well* for their particular life work. (Boston, *Documents of the School Committee, 1908*, no. 7, p. 53; quoted in Cohen and Lazerson, "Education and the Industrial Order.")

tion or tracking assignments was disguised—though not mitigated much—by another "progressive" reform: "objective" educational testing. Particularly after World War I, the capitulation of the schools to business values and concepts of efficiency led to the increased use of intelligence and scholastic achievement testing as an ostensibly unbiased means of measuring the product of schooling and classifying students.[20] The complementary growth of the guidance counseling profession allowed much of the channeling to proceed from the students' own well-counseled choices, thus adding an apparent element of voluntarism to the system.

The legacy of the progressive education movement, like the earlier reforms of the mid-nineteenth century, was a strengthened system of class stratification within schooling which continues to play an important role in the reproduction and legitimation of the social division of labor.

The class stratification of education during this period had proceeded hand in hand with the stratification of the labor force. As large bureaucratic corporations and public agencies employed an increasing fraction of all workers, a complicated segmentation of the labor force evolved, reflecting the hierarchical structure of the social relations of production. A large middle group of employees developed, comprising clerical, sales, bookkeeping, and low-level supervisory workers.[21] People holding these occupations ordinarily had a modicum of control over their own work; in some cases they directed the work of others, while themselves under the direction of higher management. The social division of labor had become a finely articulated system of work relations dominated at the top by a small group with control over work processes and a high degree of personal autonomy in their work activities, and proceeding by finely differentiated stages down the chain of bureaucratic command to workers who labored more as extensions of the machinery than as autonomous human beings.

One's status, income, and personal autonomy came to depend in great measure on one's place in the work hierarchy. And in turn, positions in the social division of labor came to be associated with educational credentials reflecting the number of years of schooling and the quality of education received. The increasing importance of

[20] R. Callahan, *Education and the Cult of Efficiency* (Chicago: University of Chicago Press, 1962); Cohen and Lazerson, "Education and the Industrial Order"; and Cremin, *Transformation of the School.*

[21] See M. Reich, "The Evolution of the U.S. Labor Force," in *The Capitalist System,* ed. R. Edwards, M. Reich, and T. Weisskopf (Englewood Cliffs, N.J.: Prentice-Hall, Inc., 1971).

schooling as a mechanism for allocating children to positions in the
class structure played a major part in legitimizing the structure itself.[22] But at the same time, it undermined the simple processes
which in the past had preserved the position and privilege of the
upper-class families from generation to generation. In short, it undermined the processes serving to reproduce the social division of
labor.

In pre-capitalist societies, direct inheritance of occupational position is common. Even in the early capitalist economy, prior to the
segmentation of the labor force on the basis of differential skills and
education, the class structure was reproduced generation after generation simply through the inheritance of physical capital by the
offspring of the capitalist class. Now that the social division of labor
is differentiated by types of competence and educational credentials
as well as by ownership of capital, the problem of inheritance is not
nearly so simple. The crucial complication arises because education
and skills are embedded in human beings; unlike physical capital,
these assets cannot be passed on to one's children at death. In an
advanced capitalist society in which education and skills play an
important role in the hierarchy of production, then, the absence of
confiscatory inheritance laws is not enough to reproduce the social
division of labor from generation to generation. Skills and educational credentials must somehow be passed on within the family. It
is a fundamental theme of this essay that schools play an important
part in reproducing and legitimizing this modern form of class
structure.

CLASS INEQUALITIES IN U.S.
SCHOOLS

Unequal schooling reproduces the social division of labor. Children whose parents occupy positions at the top of the occupational
hierarchy receive more years of schooling than working-class children. Both the amount and the content of their education greatly
facilitates their movement into positions similar to those of their
parents.

Because of the relative ease of measurement, inequalities in years
of schooling are particularly evident. If we define social-class standing by the income, occupation, and educational level of the parents,

---

[22] The role of schooling in legitimizing the class structure is spelled out in S.
Bowles, "Contradictions in U.S. Higher Education," mimeograph, 1971.

a child from the 90th percentile in the class distribution may expect on the average to achieve over four and a half more years of schooling than a child from the 10th percentile.[23] As can be seen in Table 1, social-class inequalities in the number of years of schooling received arise in part because a disproportionate number of children

TABLE 1   PERCENTAGE OF MALE CHILDREN AGED 16–17 ENROLLED IN PUBLIC SCHOOL, AND PERCENTAGE AT LESS THAN THE MODAL GRADE LEVEL, BY PARENT'S EDUCATION AND INCOME, 1960[a]

Parent's Education	Enrolled in Public School	Below Modal Level
Less than 8 years		
Family income:		
less than $3,000	66.1	47.4
$3,000–4,999	71.3	35.7
$5,000–6,999	75.5	28.3
$7,000 and over	77.1	21.8
8–11 years		
Family income:		
less than $3,000	78.6	25.0
$3,000–4,999	82.9	20.9
$5,000–6,999	84.9	16.9
$7,000 and over	86.1	13.0
12 years or more		
Family income:		
less than $3,000	89.5	13.4
$3,000–4,999	90.7	12.4
$5,000–6,999	92.1	9.7
$7,000 and over	94.2	6.9

[a] According to Census definitions, for 16-year-olds 9th grade or less and for 17-year-olds 10th grade or less define as below the modal level. Father's education is indicated if father is present; otherwise mother's education is indicated.

Source: U.S. Bureau of the Census, *Census of Population, 1960*, vol. PC-(2)5a, Table 5.

[23] The data for this calculation refer to white males who were aged 25–34 in 1962. See S. Bowles, "Schooling and Inequality from Generation to Generation" (Paper presented at the Far Eastern Meetings of the Econometric Society, Tokyo, 1970).

[24] Table 1 understates the degree of of social-class inequality in school attendance because a substantial portion of upper-income children not enrolled in public schools attend private schools. Private schools provide a parallel educational system for the upper class. I have not given much attention to these institutions as they are not quantitatively very significant in the total picture. Moreover, to deal extensively with them might detract attention from the task of explaining class inequalities in the ostensibly egalitarian portion of our school system.

28   *Samuel Bowles*

TABLE 2 COLLEGE ATTENDANCE IN 1967 AMONG HIGH SCHOOL GRADUATES, BY FAMILY INCOME[a]

Family Income[b]	Percent Who Did Not Attend College
less than $3,000	80.2
$3,000–3,999	67.7
$4,000–5,999	63.7
$6,000–7,499	58.9
$7,500–9,999	49.0
$10,000–14,999	38.7
$15,000 and over	13.3

[a] Refers to individuals who were high school seniors in October 1965 and who subsequently graduated from high school. 53.1 percent of all such students did not attend college.

[b] Family income for 12 months preceding October 1965.

Source: U.S. Bureau of the Census, *Current Population Report*, Series P–20, no. 185, 11 July 1969, p. 6. College attendance refers to both two- and four-year institutions.

from poorer families do not complete high school.[24] Table 2 indicates that these inequalities are exacerbated by social-class inequalities in college attendance among those children who did graduate from high school: even among those who had graduated from high school, children of families earning less than $3,000 per year were over six times as likely *not* to attend college as were the children of families earning over $15,000.[25]

Because schooling, especially at the college level, is heavily subsidized by the general taxpayer, those children who attend school longer have access for this reason alone to a far larger amount of public resources than those who are forced out of school or who drop out early.[26] But social-class inequalities in public expenditure on education are far more severe than the degree of inequality in years of schooling would suggest. In the first place, per-student public expenditure in four-year colleges greatly exceeds that in elementary schools; those who stay in school longer receive an increasingly large *annual* public subsidy.[27] Second, even at the elementary level,

[25] For recent evidence on these points, see U.S. Bureau of the Census, *Current Population Reports* (Series P–20), nos. 183 and 185.

[26] W. L. Hansen and B. Weisbrod, "The Distribution of Costs and Direct Benefits of Public Higher Education: the Case of California," *Journal of Human Resources* 5, no. 3 (Summer 1970): 361–370.

[27] In the school year 1969–70, per-pupil expenditures of federal, state, and local funds were $1,490 for colleges and universities and $747 for primary and secondary schools. U.S. Office of Education, *Digest of Educational Statistics, 1969* (Washington, D.C.: Government Printing Office, 1969).

schools attended by children of the poor tend to be less well endowed with equipment, books, teachers, and other inputs into the educational process. Evidence on the relationship between the level of school inputs and the income of the neighborhoods that the schools serve is presented in Table 3.[28] The data in this table indicate that both school expenditures and more direct measures of school quality vary directly with the income levels of the communities in which the school is located.

TABLE 3   INEQUALITIES IN ELEMENTARY SCHOOL RESOURCES: PERCENT DIFFERENCE IN RESOURCE AVAILABILITY ASSOCIATED WITH A ONE PERCENT DIFFERENCE IN MEAN NEIGHBORHOOD FAMILY INCOME

Resource	Within Cities 1	Between Cities 2
Current real education expenditure per student	n.a.	.73[b]
Average real elementary schoolteacher salary	.20[a]	.69[b]
Teacher-student ratio	.24[a]	n.a.
Real expenditure per pupil on teacher salary	.43[a]	n.a.
Verbal ability of teacher	.11[a]	1.20[a]

[a] John D. Owen, "The Distribution of Educational Resources in Large American cities," *Journal of Human Resources* 7, no. 1 (Winter 1972): 26–38.

[b] John D. Owen, "Towards a Public Employment Wage Theory: Some Econometric Evidence on Teacher Quality," *Industrial Labor Relations Review* 25, no. 2 (January 1972): 213–222.

Inequalities in schooling are not simply a matter of differences in years of schooling attained or in resources devoted to each student per year of schooling. Differences in the internal structure of schools themselves and in the content of schooling reflect the differences in the social-class compositions of the student bodies. The social relations of the educational process ordinarily mirror the social relations of the work roles into which most students are likely to move. Differences in rules, expected modes of behavior, and opportunities for choice are most glaring when we compare levels of schooling. Note the wide range of choice over curriculum, life style, and allocation of time afforded to college students, compared with the obedience and respect for authority expected in high school. Differentiation occurs also within each level of schooling. One needs only to compare the social relations of a junior college with those of an elite

[28] See also P. C. Sexton, *Education and Income* (New York: Viking Press, 1961).

four-year college,[29] or those of a working-class high school with those of a wealthy suburban high school, for verification of this point.[30]

The various socialization patterns in schools attended by students of different social classes do not arise by accident. Rather, they stem from the fact that the educational objectives and expectations of both parents and teachers, and the responsiveness of students to various patterns of teaching and control, differ for students of different social classes.[31] Further, class inequalities in school socialization patterns are reinforced by the inequalities in financial resources documented above. The paucity of financial support for the education of children from working-class families not only leaves more resources to be devoted to the children of those with commanding roles in the economy; it forces upon the teachers and school administrators in the working-class schools a type of social relations which fairly closely mirrors that of the factory. Thus, financial considerations in poorly supported working-class schools militate against small intimate classes, against a multiplicity of elective courses and specialized teachers (except disciplinary personnel), and preclude the amounts of free time for the teachers and free space required for a more open, flexible educational environment. The lack of financial support all but requires that students be treated as raw materials on a production line; it places a high premium on obedience and punctuality; there are few opportunities for independent, creative work or individualized attention by teachers. The well-financed schools attended by the children of the rich can offer much greater opportunities for the development of the capacity for sustained independent work and the other characteristics required for adequate job performance in the upper levels of the occupational hierarchy.

Much of the inequality in American education exists between schools, but even within a given school different children receive different educations. Class stratification within schools is achieved through tracking, differential participation in extracurricular activities, and in the attitudes of teachers and guidance personnel who

[29] See J. Binstock, "Survival in the American College Industry" mimeograph, 1971.

[30] E. Z. Friedenberg, *Coming of Age in America* (New York: Random House, 1965). It is consistent with this pattern that the play-oriented, child-centered pedagogy of the progressive movement found little acceptance outside of private schools and public schools in wealthy communities. See Cohen and Lazerson, "Education and the Industrial Order."

[31] That working-class parents seem to favor more authoritarian educational methods is perhaps a reflection of their own work experiences which have demonstrated that submission to authority is an essential ingredient in one's ability to get and hold a steady, well-paying job.

expect working-class children to do poorly, to terminate schooling early, and to end up in jobs similar to those of their parents.[32]

Not surprisingly, the results of schooling differ greatly for children of different social classes. The differing educational objectives implicit in the social relations of schools attended by children of different social classes has already been mentioned. Less important but more easily measured are differences in scholastic achievement. If we measure the output of schooling by scores on nationally standardized achievement tests, children whose parents were themselves highly educated outperform children of parents with less education by a wide margin. A recent study revealed, for example, that among white high school seniors, those whose parents were in the top education decile were on the average well over three grade levels ahead of those whose parents were in the bottom decile.[33] Although a good part of this discrepancy is the result of unequal treatment in school and unequal educational resources, much of it is related to differences in the early socialization and home environment of the children.

Given the great social-class differences in scholastic achievement, class inequalities in college attendance are to be expected. Thus one might be tempted to argue that the data in Table 1 are simply a reflection of unequal scholastic achievement in high school and do not reflect any *additional* social-class inequalities peculiar to the process of college admission. This view, so comforting to the admissions personnel in our elite universities, is unsupported by the available data, some of which is presented in Table 4. Access to a college education is highly unequal, even for children of the same measured "academic ability."

The social-class inequalities in our school system and the role they play in the reproduction of the social division of labor are too evident to be denied. Defenders of the educational system are forced back on the assertion that things are getting better, that inequalities of the past were far worse. And, indeed, some of the inequalities of the past have undoubtedly been mitigated. Yet, new inequalities

---

[32] See, for example, A. B. Hollingshead, *Elmtown's Youth* (New York: John Wiley, 1949); W. L. Warner and P. S. Lunt, *The Social Life of a Modern Community* (New Haven: Yale University Press, 1941); R. Rosenthal and L. Jacobson, *Pygmalion in the Classroom* (New York: Holt, Rinehart, and Winston, 1968); and W. E. Schafer, C. Olexa, and K. Polk, "Programmed for Social Class: Tracking in High School," *Trans-action* 7, no. 12 (October 1970): pp. 39–46.

[33] Calculation based on data in James S. Coleman et al. *Equality of Educational Opportunity*, vol. 2 (Washington, D.C.: U.S. Office of Education, 1966), and methods described in S. Bowles, "Schooling and Inequality from Generation to Generation."

TABLE 4   PROBABILITY OF COLLEGE ENTRY FOR A MALE WHO HAS
REACHED GRADE 11

		Socioeconomic Quartiles[a]			
		Low 1	2	3	High 4
	Low 1	.06	.12	.13	.26
	2	.13	.15	.29	.36
Ability					
Quartiles[a]	3	.25	.34	.45	.65
	High 4	.48	.70	.73	.87

[a] The socioeconomic index is a composite measure including family income, father's occupation and education, mother's education, etc. The ability scale is a composite of tests measuring general academic aptitude.
   Source: Based on a large sample of U.S. high school students as reported in John C. Flannagan and William W. Cooley, *Project TALENT, One-Year Follow-Up Studies*, Cooperative Research Project No. 2333, School of Education, University of Pittsburgh, 1966.

have apparently developed to take their place, for the available historical evidence lends little support to the idea that our schools are on the road to equality of educational opportunity. For example, data from a recent U.S. Census survey reported in Table 5 indicate that graduation from college has become increasingly dependent on one's class background. This is true despite the fact that the probability of high school graduation is becoming increasingly equal across social classes. On balance, the available data suggest that the number of years of schooling attained by a child depends upon the social-class standing of his father at least as much in the recent period as it did fifty years ago.[34]

   The argument that our "egalitarian" education compensates for inequalities generated elsewhere in the capitalist system is so patently fallacious that few persist in maintaining it. But the discrepancy between the ideology and the reality of the U.S. school system is far greater than would appear from a passing glance at the above data. In the first place, if education is to compensate for the social-

[34] See P. M. Blau and O. D. Duncan, *The American Occupational Structure* (New York: Wiley, 1967). More recent data do not contradict the evidence of no trend toward equality. A 1967 Census survey, the most recent available, shows that among high school graduates in 1965, the probability of college attendance for those whose parents had attended college has continued to rise relative to the probability of college attendance for those whose parents had attended less than eight years of school. See U.S. Bureau of the Census, *Current Population Reports* (Series P-20), no. 185, 11 July 1969.

TABLE 5 AMONG SONS WHO HAD REACHED HIGH SCHOOL, PERCENTAGE WHO GRADUATED FROM COLLEGE, BY SON'S AGE AND FATHER'S LEVEL OF EDUCATION

Son's Age in 1962	Likely Dates of College Graduation[a]	Father's Education						
		Less than 8 Years	Some High School		High School Graduate		Some College or More	
			Percent Graduating	Ratio to <8	Percent Graduating	Ratio to <8	Percent Graduating	Ratio to <8
25–34	1950–59	7.6	17.4	2.29	25.6	3.37	51.9	6.83
35–44	1940–49	8.6	11.9	1.38	25.3	2.94	53.9	6.27
45–54	1930–39	7.7	9.8	1.27	15.1	1.96	36.9	4.79
55–64	1920–29	8.9	9.8	1.10	19.2	2.16	29.8	3.35

[a] Assuming college graduation at age 22

Source: Based on U.S. Census data as reported in William G. Spady, "Educational Mobility and Access: Growth and Paradoxes," *American Journal of Sociology* 73, no. 3 (November 1967): 273–86.

class immobility caused by the inheritance of wealth and privilege, education must be structured so as to yield a negative correlation between social-class background of the child and the quantity and quality of his schooling. Thus the assertion that education compensates for inequalities in inherited wealth and privilege is falsified not so much by the extent of the social-class inequalities in the school system as by their very existence, or, more correctly, by the absence of compensatory inequalities.

Moreover, if we turn from the problem of intergenerational immobility to the problem of inequality of income at a given moment, a similar argument applies. In a capitalist economy, the increasing importance of schooling in the economy exercises a disequalizing tendency on the distribution of income even in the absence of social-class inequalities in quality and quantity of schooling. To see why this is so, consider a simple capitalist economy in which only two factors are used in production: uneducated and undifferentiated labor, and capital, the ownership of which is unequally distributed among the population. The only source of income inequality in this society is the unequal distribution of capital. As the labor force becomes differentiated by type of skill or schooling, inequalities in labor earnings contribute to total income inequality, augmenting the inequalities inherent in the concentration of capital. This will be the case even if education and skills are distributed randomly among the population. The disequalizing tendency will of course be intensified if the owners of capital also acquire a disproportionate amount of those types of education and training which confer access to high-paying jobs.[35] A substantial negative correlation between

---

[35] A simple statistical model will elucidate the main relationships involved.

Let y (individual or family income) be the sum of w (earnings from labor, including embodied education and skills, L) and k (earnings from capital, K), related according to the equation $y = w + k = aK^A L^B$. The coefficients A and B represent the relative importance of capital and labor as sources of income. The variance of the logarithm of income (a common measure of inequality) can then be represented by the following expression:

$$\text{var log } y = A^2 \text{var log } K + B^2 \text{var log } L + 2AB \text{ covar (log } L, \text{ log } K).$$

The first term on the right represents the contribution of inequalities in capital ownership to total inequality, the second measures that part of total income inequality due to inequalities of education and skills embodied in labor, and the third represents the contribution to income inequality of social class inequalities in the supply of skills and schooling. Prior to the educational differentiation of the labor force, the variance of labor was zero. All workers were effectively equal. The variance of the logarithm of income would then be due entirely to capital inequality and would be exactly equal to $A^2 \text{var log } K$. The rise of education as a source of income and labor differentiation will increase the variance of the logarithm of embodied labor unless all workers receive identical education and train-the ownership of capital and the quality and quantity of schooling received would have been required merely to neutralize the disequalizing effect of the rise of schooling as an economic phenomenon. And while some research has minimized the importance of social-class biases in schooling,[36] nobody has yet suggested that class and schooling were inversely related!

CLASS CULTURE AND CLASS POWER

The pervasive and persistent inequalities in American education would seem to refute an interpretation of education that asserts its egalitarian functions. But the facts of inequality do not by themselves suggest an alternate explanation. Indeed, they pose serious problems of interpretation. If the costs of education borne by students and their families were very high, or if nepotism were rampant, or if formal segregation of pupils by social class were practiced, or if educational decisions were made by a select few whom we might call the power elite, it would not be difficult to explain the continued inequalities in U.S. education. The problem of interpretation, however, is to reconcile the above empirical findings with the facts of our society as we perceive them: public and virtually tuition-free education at all levels, few legal instruments for the direct implementation of class segregation, a limited role for "contacts" or nepotism in the achievement of high status or income, a commitment (at the rhetorical level at least) to equality of educational opportunity, and a system of control of education which, if not particularly democratic, extends far beyond anything resembling a power elite. The attempt to reconcile these apparently discrepant facts leads to a consideration of the social division of labor, the associated class cultures, and the exercise of class power.

I will argue that the social division of labor—based on the hierarchical structure of production—gives rise to distinct class subcultures. The values, personality traits, and expectations characteristic

---

ing. This is true even if the third term is zero, indicating no social class inequalities in the provision of skills and education.

To assert the conventional faith in the egalitarian influence of the rising economic importance of education, one would have to argue that the rise of education is likely to be associated with either (1) a fall in *A*, the relative importance of capital as a source of earnings; (2) a decrease in the size of the covariance of of logarithms of capital and labor; (3) a decrease in the inequality of capital ownerships; or (4) an increase in equality in the supply of education. While each is possible, I see no compelling reason why education should *produce* these results.

[36] See, for example, Robert Hauser, "Educational Stratification in the United States," *Sociological Inquiry* 40 (Spring 1970): 102–29.

of each subculture are transmitted from generation to generation
through class differences in family socialization and complementary
differences in the type and amount of schooling ordinarily attained
by children of various class positions. These class differences in
schooling are maintained in large measure through the capacity of
the upper class to control the basic principles of school finance,
pupil evaluation, and educational objectives. This outline, and
what follows, is put forward as an interpretation, consistent where
testable with the available data, though lacking as yet in firm empirical support for some important links in the argument.

The social relations of production characteristic of advanced
capitalist societies (and many socialist societies) are most clearly il-
lustrated in the bureaucracy and hierarchy of the modern corporation.[37] Occupational roles in the capitalist economy may be grouped
according to the degree of independence and control exercised by
the person holding the job. Some evidence exists that the personality attributes associated with the adequate performance of jobs in
occupational categories defined in this broad way differ considerably, some apparently requiring independence and internal discipline, and others emphasizing such traits as obedience, predictabil-
ity, and willingness to subject oneself to external controls.[38]

These personality attributes are developed primarily at a young
age, both in the family and, to a lesser extent, in secondary socializing institutions such as schools.[39] Because people tend to marry
within their own class (in part because spouses often meet in our
class-segregated schools), both parents are likely to have a similar
set of these fundamental personality traits. Thus, children of parents
occupying a given position in the occupational hierarchy grow up in
homes where child-rearing methods and perhaps even the physical
surroundings tend to develop personality characteristics appropriate to adequate job performance in the occupational roles of the parents.[40] The children of managers and professionals are taught self-

[37] Max Weber referred to bureaucracy as the "most rational offspring" of discipline, and remarked: ". . . military discipline is the ideal model for the modern
capitalist factory. . . ." See "The Meaning of Discipline," reprinted in H. H.
Gerth and C. W. Mills, eds. *From Max Weber: Essays in Sociology* (New York:
Oxford University Press, 1958), p. 261.

[38] For a survey of the literature see J. P. Robinson, R. Athanasiou, and K.
Head. "Measures of Occupational Attitudes and Occupational Characteristics"
(Survey Research Center, University of Michigan, February 1969).

[39] See, for example, Benjamin Bloom, *Stability and Change in Human Characteristics* (New York: Wiley, 1964).

[40] Note, for example, the class differences in child rearing with respect to the
importance of obedience. See M. Kohn, "Social Class and Parental Values," in *The*

reliance within a broad set of constraints;[41] the children of production-line workers are taught obedience.

Although this relation between parents' class position and child's personality attributes operates primarily in the home, it is reinforced by schools and other social institutions. Thus, to take an example introduced earlier, the authoritarian social relations of working-class high schools complement the discipline-oriented early socialization patterns experienced by working-class children. The relatively greater freedom of wealthy suburban schools extends and formalizes the early independence training characteristic of upper-class families.

Schools reinforce other aspects of family socialization as well. The aspirations and expectations of students and parents concerning both the type and the amount of schooling are strongly related to social class.[42] The expectations of teachers, guidance counselors, and school administrators ordinarily reinforce those of the students and parents. Schools often encourage students to develop aspirations and expectations typical of their social class, even if the child tends to have "deviant" aspirations.

It is true that to some extent schools introduce common elements of socialization for all students regardless of social class. Discipline, respect for property, competition, and punctuality are part of the

Family, ed. R. Coser (New York: St. Martin's Press, 1964); and L. Dolger and J. Ginandes, "Children's Attitudes towards Discipline as Related to Socioeconomic Status," *Journal of Experimental Education* 15, no. 2 (December 1946): 161–165. See also the study of differences in child-rearing practices in families headed by bureaucrats as opposed to entrepreneurs by D. Miller and G. Swanson, *The Changing American Parent* (New York: Wiley, 1958). Also, E. E. Maccoby, P. K. Gibbs, et al., "Methods of Child-Rearing in Two Social Classes," in *Readings in Child Development,* ed. W. E. Martin and C. B. Stendler (New York: Harcourt Brace, 1954). While the existence of class differences in child rearing is supported by most of the available data (but see H. Lewis, "Child-Rearing Among Low-Income Families," in *Poverty in America,* ed. L. Ferman et al. [Ann Arbor, Michigan: University of Michigan Press, 1965]), the stability of these differences over time has been questioned by U. Bronfenbrenner, "Socialization and Social Class through Time and Space," in *Education and Society,* ed. W. W. Kallenbach and H. M. Hodges (Columbus, Ohio: C. E. Merrill, 1963).

[41] See M. Winterbottom, "The Sources of Achievement Motivation in Mothers' Attitudes toward Independence Training," in *The Achievement Motive,* ed. D. C. McClelland et al. (New York: Appleton-Century-Crofts, 1953); and M. Kohn, "Social Class and Parent-Child Relationships: An Interpretation," *American Journal of Sociology* 68, no. 4 (January 1963): 471–480.

[42] See, for example, S. M. Lipset and R. Bendix, *Social Mobility in Industrial Society* (Berkeley, Calif.: University of California Press, 1959); and T. Iwand and J. Stoyle, "Social Rigidity: Income and Occupational Choice in Rural Pennsylvania," *Economic and Business Bulletin* 22 (Spring-Summer 1970): 25–30.

implicit curriculum of virtually all schools. Yet, given the existing institutional arrangements, the ability of a school to change a child's personality, values, and expectations is severely limited. The responsiveness of children to different types of schooling seems to depend importantly upon the types of personality traits, values, and expectations developed through the family. Furthermore, children spend a small amount of time in school—less than one-quarter of their waking hours over the course of a year. Thus schools are probably more effective when they attempt to complement and reinforce rather than to oppose the socialization processes of the home and neighborhood. It is not surprising, then, that social-class differences in scholastic achievement and other measures of school success are far greater than would be accounted for by differences in the measured school financial resources and other inputs (quality and quantity of teachers, etc.) alone.[43]

In this interpretation class differences in the total effect of schooling are primarily the result of differences in what I have called class subculture. The educational system serves less to change the results of the primary socialization in the home than to ratify them and render them in adult form. The complementary relationship between family socialization and schools serves to reproduce patterns of class culture from generation to generation.

The operation of the labor market translates differences in class culture into income inequalities and occupational hierarchies. The personality traits, values, and expectations characteristic of different class cultures play a major role in determining an individual's success in gaining a high income or prestigious occupation. The apparent contribution of schooling to occupational success and higher income seems to be explained primarily by the personality characteristics of those who have higher educational attainments.[44] Although the rewards to intellectual capacities are quite limited in the labor market (except for a small number of high-level jobs), mental abilities are important in getting ahead in school. Grades, the probability of continuing to higher levels of schooling, and a host of other

[43] S. Bowles, "Toward an Educational Production Function," in *Education, Income, and Human Capital,* ed. W. L. Hansen (New York: National Bureau of Economic Research, 1970).

[44] This view is elaborated in H. Gintis, "Education, Technology, and Worker Productivity," *American Economic Association Proceedings* 61, no. 2 (May 1971): 266–279. For other studies stressing the noncognitive dimensions of the schooling experience, see T. Parsons, "The School Class as a Social System: Some of Its Functions in American Society," *Harvard Educational Review* 29, no. 4 (Fall 1959): 297–318; and R. Dreeben, *On What Is Learned in School* (Reading, Mass.: Addison Wesley, 1968).

school success variables are positively correlated with "objective" measures of intellectual capacities. Partly for this reason, one's experience in school reinforces the belief that promotion and rewards are distributed fairly. The close relationship between educational attainments and later occupational success thus provides a meritocratic appearance to mask the mechanisms that reproduce the class system from generation to generation.

So far, the perpetuation of inequality through the schooling system has been represented as an almost automatic, self-enforcing mechanism, operating only through the medium of class culture. An important further dimension of the interpretation is added if we note that positions of control in the productive hierarchy tend to be associated with positions of political influence. Given the disproportionate share of political power held by the upper class and their capacity to determine the accepted patterns of behavior and procedures, to define the national interest, and in general to control the ideological and institutional context in which educational decisions are made, it is not surprising to find that resources are allocated unequally among school tracks, between schools serving different classes, and between levels of schooling. The same configuration of power results in curricula, methods of instruction, and criteria of selection and promotion that confer benefits disproportionately on the children of the upper class.

It is not asserted here that the upper class controls the main decision-making bodies in education, although a good case could probably be made that this is so. The power of the upper class is hypothesized as existing in its capacity to define and maintain a set of rules of operation or decision criteria—"rules of the game"—which, though often seemingly innocuous and sometimes even egalitarian in their ostensible intent, have the effect of maintaining the unequal system.

The operation of two prominent examples of these rules of the game will serve to illustrate the point. The first important principle is that excellence in schooling should be rewarded. Given the capacity of the upper class to define excellence in terms on which upper-class children tend to excel (e.g., scholastic achievement), adherence to this principle yields inegalitarian outcomes (e.g., unequal access to higher education) while maintaining the appearance of fair treatment.[45] Thus the principle of rewarding excellence serves to

[45] Those who would defend the "reward excellence" principle on the grounds of efficient selection to ensure the most efficient use of educational resources might ask themselves: Why should colleges admit those with the highest college entrance examination board scores? Why not the lowest, or the middle? According to con-

40   *Samuel Bowles*

legitimize the unequal consequences of schooling by associating
success with competence. At the same time, the institution of objectively administered tests of performance serves to allow a limited
amount of upward mobility among exceptional children of the lower
class, thus providing further legitimation of the operations of the
social system by giving some credence to the myth of widespread
mobility.

The second example is the principle that elementary and secondary schooling should be financed in very large measure from local
revenues. This principle is supported on the grounds that it is necessary to preserve political liberty. Given the degree of residential
segregation by income level, the effect of this principle is to produce
an unequal distribution of school resources among children of different classes. Towns with a large tax base can spend large sums for
the education of their disproportionately upper-class children, without suffering a higher-than-average tax rate.[46] Because the main
resource inequalities in schooling thus exist between, rather than
within, school districts,[47] and because no effective mechanism exists
for redistribution of school funds among school districts, poor families lack a viable political strategy for correcting the inequality.[48]

The above rules of the game—rewarding "excellence" and financing schools locally—illustrate the complementarity between the political and economic power of the upper class. In each case, adherence to the rule has the effect of generating unequal consequences
via a mechanism that operates largely outside the political system.
As long as one adheres to the "reward excellence" principle, the
responsibility for unequal results in schooling appears to lie outside
the upper class, often in some fault of the poor—such as their class

---

ventional standards of efficiency, the rational social objective of the college is to
render the greatest *increment* in individual capacities ("value added," to the economist), not to produce the most illustrious graduating class ("gross output"). Yet
if incremental gain is the objective, it is far from obvious that choosing from the
top is the best policy.

[46] Some dimensions of this problem are discussed in S. Weiss, "Existing Disparities in Public School Finance and Proposals for Reform" (Research Report to the
Federal Reserve Bank of Boston, no. 46, February 1970).

[47] Recall that Owen, whose data appear in Table 3, found that the relationship
of various measures of teacher quality to the family income level of the area
served by the schools was considerably higher between cities than within cities.

[48] In 1969, federal funds constituted only 7 percent of the total financing of
public elementary and secondary schooling. Moreover, current distribution formulas governing state and federal expenditures are only mildly egalitarian in their
impact. See K. A. Simon and W. V. Grant, *Digest of Educational Statistics, 1969*
(Washington, D.C.: Department of Health, Education, and Welfare, 1969).

culture, which is viewed as lying beyond the reach of political action or criticism. Likewise, as long as the local financing of schools is maintained, the achievement of equality of resources among children of different social classes requires the class integration of school districts, an objective for which there are no effective political instruments as long as we allow a market in residential properties and an unequal distribution of income.

Thus, the consequences of an unequal distribution of political power among classes appear to complement the results of class culture in maintaining an educational system that has been capable of transmitting status from generation to generation, and capable in addition of political survival in the formally democratic and egalitarian environment of the contemporary United States.

The role of the schools in reproducing and legitimizing the social division of labor has recently been challenged by popular egalitarian movements. At the same time, the educational system is showing signs of internal structural weakness.[49] These two developments suggest that fundamental change in the schooling process may soon be possible. Analysis of both the potential and the limits of educational change will be facilitated by drawing together and extending the strands of our argument.

THE LIMITS OF EDUCATIONAL REFORM

If the above attempt to identify the roots of inequality in American education is convincing, it has done more than reconcile apparent discrepancies between the democratic forms and unequal content of that education. For it is precisely the sources of educational inequality which we must understand in order to develop successful political strategies in the pursuit of educational equality.

I have argued that the structure of education reflects the social relations of production. For at least the past 150 years, expansion of education and changes in the forms of schooling have been responses to needs generated by the economic system. The sources of present inequality in American education were found in the mutual reinforcement of class subcultures and social-class biases in the operations of the school system itself. The analysis strongly suggests that educational inequalities are rooted in the basic institutions of our economy. Reconsideration of some of the basic mechanisms of edu-

[40] See S. Bowles, "Contradictions in U.S. Higher Education," mimeograph, 1971.

cational inequality lends support to this proposition. First, the principle of rewarding academic excellence in educational promotion and selection serves not only to legitimize the process by which the social division of labor is reproduced. It is also a basic part of the process that socializes young people to work for external rewards and encourages them to develop motivational structures fit for the alienating work of the capitalist economy.[50] Selecting students from the bottom or the middle of the achievement scale for promotion to higher levels of schooling would go a long way toward equalizing education, but it would also jeopardize the schools' capacity to train productive and well-adjusted workers.[51] Second, the way in which local financing of schools operates to maintain educational inequality is also rooted in the capitalist economy, in this case in the existence of an unequal distribution of income, free markets in residential property, and the narrow limits of state power. It seems unwise to emphasize this aspect of the long-run problem of equality in education, however, for the inequalities in school resources resulting from the localization of finance may not be of crucial importance in maintaining inequalities in the effects of education. Moreover, a significant undermining of the principle of local finance may already be underway in response to pressures from the poorer states and school districts.

Of greater importance in the perpetuation of educational inequality are differential class subcultures. These class-based differences in personality, values, and expectations, I have argued, represent an adaptation to the different requirements of adequate work performance at various levels in the hierarchical social relations of production. Class subcultures, then, stem from the everyday experiences of workers in the structure of production characteristic of capitalist societies.

It should be clear by this point that educational equality cannot be achieved through changes in the school system alone. Nonetheless, attempts at educational reform may move us closer to that objective if, in their failure, they lay bare the unequal nature of our school system and destroy the illusion of unimpeded mobility through education. Successful educational reforms—reducing racial or class disparities in schooling, for example—may also serve the cause of equality of education, for it seems likely that equalizing access to schooling will challenge the system either to make good its

---

[50] Gintis, "Education, Technology, and Worker Productivity."
[51] Consider what would happen to the internal discipline of schools if the students' objective were to end up at the bottom of the grade distribution!

promise of rewarding educational attainment or to find ways of coping with a mass disillusionment with the great panacea.[52]

Yet, if the record of the last 150 years of educational reforms is any guide, we should not expect radical change in education to result from the efforts of those confining their attention to the schools. The political victories of past reform movements have apparently resulted in little if any effective equalization. My interpretation of the educational consequences of class culture and class power suggests that these educational reform movements failed because they sought to eliminate educational inequalities without challenging the basic institutions of capitalism.

Efforts to equalize education through changes in government policy will at best scratch the surface of inequality. For much of the inequality in American education has its origin outside the limited sphere of state power, in the hierarchy of work relations and the associated differences in class culture. As long as jobs are defined so that some have power over many and others have power over none—as long as the social division of labor persists—educational inequality will be built into society in the United States.

[52] The failure of the educational programs of the War on Poverty to raise significantly the incomes of the poor is documented in T. I. Ribich, *Education and Poverty* (Washington, D.C.: The Brookings Institution, 1968). In the case of blacks, dramatic increases in the level of schooling relative to whites have scarcely affected the incomes of blacks relative to whites. See R. Weiss, "The Effects of Education on the Earnings of Blacks and Whites," *Review of Economics and Statistics* 52, no. 2 (May 1970): 150–59. It is no wonder that Booker T. Washington's plea that blacks should educate themselves before demanding equality has lost most of its once widespread support.

I
The public school establishment

Understanding central elements of public schooling in the United States requires analysis not only of the structure of power in education but also the processes by which the establishment shapes major policies and patterns. The selection by Harmon Zeigler and Wayne Peak illustrates this type of analysis in which power and process are jointly examined. Zeigler and Peak begin by documenting a prominent feature of public education—the conservative outlook of both teachers and textbooks. They then ask why this situation is so prevalent, and they set forth several alternative hypotheses: teaching has a conservative tone because (1) there are external pressures on schools to avoid controversy, (2) schools simply "mirror" local community values, which are often conservative, or (3) internal school governance and methods of teacher recruitment encourage the avoidance of unorthodox perspectives. The authors conclude that only one of these processes primarily accounts for the conservative curriculum.

The next three selections focus on major interest groups and formal authorities centrally involved in the governance of public education. Myron Brenton discusses the politics of the two major organizations representing teachers—the National Education Association and the American Federation of Teachers. Brenton notes that even when teachers build strong organizations for advocating their collective interests, organizational effectiveness may be seriously impaired by inclusion of school administrators and by hesitancy to employ standard labor strategies such as the strike. Moreover, while teacher concerns are often consistent with the aspirations of students and the community, teacher demands can be at odds with local needs, as exemplified in the New York City struggles over community control of the schools.

Frederick Wirt and Michael Kirst survey educational politics at the state level. They provide an overview of the relative influence of and constraints on formal bodies, such as State Boards of Education and state legislatures, and the political significance of various interest groups concerned with education, particularly state affiliates of the National Education Association. Mario Fantini, Marilyn Gittell, and Richard Magat focus on the local school level and explore the interplay between the local school board, school bureaucracy, and community. They observe that much of the real authority for daily operation of the school system has slipped from the school board into the hands of the school administration.

In the final selection in this section, W. W. Charters raises a number of questions about the conclusions that have often been drawn from studies of the occupations of school board members and the social class origins of teachers and school superintendents. For instance, he challenges the assumption frequently made in such research that the occupation of a school board member necessarily colors his or her position on school policies. His cautionary criticism can be applied to many studies of elites.

chapter two

The political functions
of the educational system

HARMON ZEIGLER AND WAYNE PEAK

. . . In general, teachers are not inclined toward using the classroom as a medium for the discussion of controversial issues. While there are considerable variations in approach to the classroom, teachers find their lives much less complicated if they avoid controversy. We are referring here not only to the potential for trouble within the community, but also to the potential for trouble within the classroom. Classes are easier to manage if the authority structure is not challenged. Engaging in controversy presents a challenge to the authority structure and, therefore, is avoided.

Avoidance of controversy is reinforced by the content of texts which, for better or worse, establish the nature of the content of a course of instruction. A brief survey of the quality of public school texts in history, government, or civics indicates the Victorian attitude toward politics which is typical of American education. The main object of most texts apparently is to protect rather than to inform the minds of youths.

In 1943, Hunt and Metcalf (1943:230) listed six closed areas in social studies texts. They were:

1. Economics. Students and teachers could find little about possible shortcomings in the free enterprise system. They could certainly find nothing about the extent to which we actually have a free enterprise system.

2. Race and minority relations. There are virtually no realistic discussions of this problem.

3. Social class. In spite of obvious facts about the significance of social class in political behavior, the prevailing theme is that "there are no social classes in America."

From Harmon Zeigler and Wayne Peak, "The Political Functions of the Educational System," *Sociology of Education* 43 (Spring, 1970), pp. 129–142. Reprinted by permission of the American Sociological Association and the authors.

4. Sex, courtship, and marriage. It should come as no surprise that this subject is treated in a wholly unreal fashion.
5. Religion and morality. Texts tactfully advised teachers to avoid this subject entirely.
6. Nationalism and patriotism. Nationalism as a destructive force is not mentioned. Patriotism is unquestionably accepted as an over-arching goal, but the specific behaviors which are presumed to be patriotic are not discussed. Hence, saluting the flag is an unquestioned ritual.

From the available evidence, we conclude that Hunt and Metcalf's description is just about as valid today as it was in 1943. We cannot check each of the six closed areas as carefully as we should like, nor can we be assured that our survey is truly representative of the available texts. However, a few quotations from some widely used texts might prove helpful. Take, for example, the following statement about the American economic system:

> One needs only to look at the great achievements and the standard of living of the American people to see the advantages of our economic system. . . . We believe that a well regulated capitalism—a free choice, individual incentives, private enterprise system—is the best guarantee of the better life for all mankind (McClenoghan, 1966:20 cited in Massialas, 1967:179).

There is no discussion of any alternatives to this economic system, not even in the "some say—others say" style that characterizes some efforts to consider alternatives. Further, as Massialas (1967) notes, a picture accompanying this discussion shows people waiting in line in the rain to be treated in the English National Health Service.[1]

Race relations is regarded as a "controversial social issue" and is treated with extreme caution. While there are some texts which are more realistic than others, the following quotation is typical:

> In 1954, the United States Supreme Court made a decision stating that separate schools for Negro children were unconstitutional. This decision caused much controversy, but there has been general agreement, however, that some system must be developed to provide equal educational opportunity for all children—regardless of race, nationality, religion, or whether they live in cities or rural areas (cited in Krug, 1967:202).

Of course, this statement is patently false; but it also could allow support for the separate but equal doctrine. There is no discussion

---

[1] Much of our analysis of texts is based upon material contained in this volume. Massialas' excellent article has been particularly useful, and citations from it have been of great help in the present undertaking.

of the vigor with which Southern states resisted the order. Presumably, the students were given no explanation for the fact that race relations remain America's most divisive dilemma.

Concerning social class, sex, and religion, little can be said because the treatment of these topics is so sparse. Consider, for example, the following treatment of class (Cole and Montgomery, 1963: 365 cited in Girault, 1967:227): ". . . classes in society are more or less inevitable . . . it is important to keep the social classes open." Warner, Hollingshead, the Lynds, and, in fact, most American sociologists might never have written if this text is to be taken as evidence of their impact below the college level. Sex usually is discussed in psychology texts. Students are exposed to the arguments for and against going steady. One of the most obvious advantages, an advantage seized by the majority of those who "go steady," is, needless to say, ignored. In an age in which open cohabitation is becoming an alternative to marriage, such discussions are absurd. The treatment of religion, which occurs occasionally in sociology texts, appears to be as far removed from the sociology of religion as the treatment of sex is from the concerns of youth. Many texts assert that reason alone cannot sustain man; faith is necessary. Usually faith and Christianity are equated (Girault, 1967).

Patriotism, which is characteristic of the study of American government in the public schools, may be less jingoistic than it once was. However, texts carefully intersperse discussions of government structure (considered in purely legalistic terms) with appropriate exhortations such as: "No other country has more nearly approached the goals of true democracy as has our United States. . . . No doubt many of the early settlers were inspired men . . ." (Cole and Montgomery, 1963:341–342 cited in Girault, 1967:227); and, "Because the nations of the world have not yet learned to live permanently at peace, the United States today must maintain large defensive forces" (Ludlum, et al., 1965 cited in Massialas, 1967:180).

The treatment of the American political process is totally unreal. A single example selected from the abundance that exists should serve to make the point. One text (Ludlum, et al., 1965) devotes an entire chapter to the electoral process but fails to mention such standard sources as *The American Voter*. As Massialas (1967:182) observed: "The five main ideas of the chapter on voting are: (1) 'voting is a process that makes possible peaceful change,' (2) 'voting promotes citizen participation in government,' (3) 'voting helps to promote equality,' (4) 'voting promotes obedience to government,' and (5) 'voting promotes the self-respect of every individual.' "

The manner in which texts treat communism is even more as-

tonishing. In both the "challenge of communism" courses which
have become quite popular recently and in the general civics
courses, communism is pictured as a total evil. Most state departments of education primarily are concerned with demonstrating the
fallacies of communism rather than encouraging objective comparison. An unswerving ruthless conspiracy dominated by the Soviet
Union (texts have not yet discovered the shift toward China as the
source of all evil) is the image which is presented, almost without
exception. Texts warn students that they will be "badly fooled" if
they "take the Russians at their word"; the "errors" of Marx are
listed (no communist sources are cited); and the contrast of good
versus evil is made quite explicit. In the remote event that the
student fails to get the message, end of chapter assignments, maps,
and other visual aids are equally biased (Brown and Pelthier, 1964:
20–21, cited in Massialas, 1967:183). For instance, four projects accompanying one text are: (1) Write a short paper on agreements
with other nations broken by the Soviet Union; (2) Draw a chart
contrasting the way of life in a democracy and in totalitarian government; (3) Organize a panel to discuss United States Policy toward Cuba (preceded by the statement, "The presence of a communist dictatorship in Cuba poses a threat to the peace of the Western
Hemisphere"); (4) Compile a list of Marx's errors.

To provide a sense of geographical continuity, maps frequently
are included in social studies texts. One such map divides the world
into four camps: The United States, the communist bloc, the un-
committed nations, and the Free World—including Spain, Portugal,
Formosa, and Haiti. (Presumably, "free" is a synonym for degree of
friendliness with the United States rather than a description of the
internal politics of a country.) If, given the boredom which might be
expected to accompany class discussions of such simplistic notions,
the class still has not figured out how to get a good grade, the final
assignment should reduce any remaining ambiguities: "List as many
criticisms of communism as you can" (McClenoghan, 1966, cited in
Massialas, 1967:184).

Since most social studies teachers are not trained to distinguish
facts from values and, in any case, probably find most of the anti-
communism and ethnocentrism of the texts quite compatible with
their own values, little contrary information filters into the classroom. Furthermore, since such unreal descriptions are reinforced by
other sources of information (mass media and family), it is possible
that our attention should be directed away from attitude change
and toward attitude organization.

The notion of attitude organization, as developed by Jules Henry
(1957), consists of grouping and focusing poorly articulated atti-

tudes. Given the goals of the educational system, its success might be better measured in terms of providing order to attitudes and directing them toward larger social goals, such as the maintenance of positive attitudes toward national symbols. We suspect, however, that the crude indoctrination typical of texts is less effective in achieving organization than is the more subtle learning experiences manifested by means of teacher-student interaction and the norms of school organization. Furthermore, the consequences of the social studies curriculum might operate, in the long run, to increase cynicism rather than trust. Jennings and Niemi (1968:178) argue that the social studies curriculum—in postponing an encounter with the realities of political life—makes an increase in cynicism a natural consequence of the departure from high school. They find a "rather sharp rise in the level of cynicism as high school seniors move ahead in a few years into the adult world."

There is also the possibility that cynicism is latent in the high school population and, therefore, is released from constraint when adulthood is reached. Teachers, in keeping with the general norms of public education, are overly concerned with authority. The style of teaching, emphasizing the authority of the teacher, may seem to some students to be in contrast with the democratic norms which comprise the official ideology. The available evidence, such as that presented in Table 1, strongly suggests that teachers are not capable of conducting an interaction with a student on an equal basis. Some of the data collected by Jennings and Zeigler is suggestive of the atmosphere of the class.

TABLE 1   ATTITUDES OF TEACHERS TOWARD AUTHORITY

Item	Per Cent Agree	Per Cent Disagree
Children should be given greater freedom in expressing their natural impulses and desires, even if these impulses are frowned upon by people.	42	58
Schools should return to the practice of administering a good spanking when other methods fail.	59	41
A good teacher never lets students address him or her except as Mr., Miss, or Mrs.	75	25
What youth needs most is strict discipline, rugged determination, and the will to work and fight for family and country.	69	31
The main purpose of social studies courses is to teach students to be good citizens.	88	12
Obedience and respect for authority are the most important virtues children should learn.	60	40
Students today don't respect their teachers enough.	57	43

In Table 1 a few items which have yet to be analyzed systematically give some evidence of the concerns of teachers. While we do not know much about the actual behavior of teachers, we might assume that such attitudes provide a strong propensity for creating a rigid classroom situation. Furthermore, in spite of the shibboleths of texts, to which teachers undoubtedly pay lip service, teachers appear to be as unclear about the application of democratic ideals to concrete situations as is the general population. A minority believe that police should not have the power to censor books and movies; a majority do not wish to provide First Amendment freedom to social or political nonconformists (Weiser and Hayes, 1966:477–478).

Since teachers are part of the educational grouping generally presumed to be the staunchest supporters of civil liberties, their attitudes are in conflict with what we have learned about the role of education in contributing to the open mind. However, teachers are part of an authoritarian system and develop appropriate occupational values (Jennings and Zeigler, 1969:77–79). This comment leads directly into our final section, but first there is the need to note the apparent contradiction between what we are saying and the evidence presented by Almond and Verba (1963:332–334). Forty percent of their American adult respondents remembered participating in class discussions and debating political issues in school, in contrast with only 16 percent of the British respondents and slightly fewer of the respondents in other countries. Two comments seem to be in order. First, a majority of adults do *not* recall participation, a fact which should be placed against the context of America's cultural emphases (as contrasted with those of England). Second, if the nature of the discussion resembled the study guides as set forth in texts, such discussions simply served to provide peer group reinforcement of prevailing ideologies.

THE CONTROLLERS OF EDUCATION

Why is the situation as it has been described? Three possible explanations come most readily to mind. First, and certainly the most popular, is the "pressure group" argument. Schools are described as the victims of unrelenting pressure from extremist groups who keep a sharp lookout for deviations from the majoritarian ideology. Second, there is the assumption that schools mirror the dominant values of the society they serve and, therefore, can be expected to be replicas of the value structure of the society. Third, there is the argument that schools, because of the structure under which they are governed and because of patterns of occupational recruitment and socialization, are of necessity institutions that function to set limits to the legitimacy of policy alternatives. While each argument has some truth in it, we find the third more in keeping with the facts as we see them.

PRESSURE GROUPS

The pressure group argument collects information about cases in which teachers have become the focus of community controversy because of the manner in which they conduct their classes. However, a review of this literature does not tell one about the relative frequency of such attacks. When attacks occur, they are indeed spectacular. However, relative to the total amount of interaction between teachers, students, and the community, the activity of pressure groups seems to be relatively minor. This is not to suggest that pressure, when it is exerted, is not effective. One well publicized case may be enough to constrain many more teachers than those personally involved in the dispute. Nevertheless, there is virtually no evidence concerning the extent to which the demands of interest groups are communicated to administrators and teachers, and the extent to which demands can be linked to decisions regarding the values of the interest groups.

The principal author's own evidence indicates that teachers are not especially aware of—nor concerned about—the activities of interest groups (Zeigler, 1967:128–130). Administrators, on the other hand, are more sensitive to group demands. Therefore, it is possible that administrators, who have more immediate access to the weapons of sanction and who are viewed by teachers as a more potent threat, serve as transmission belts between interest groups and teachers. Such a possibility is given some credence because of the tendency of administrators to avoid conflict whenever possible. Thus they are likely to try to satisfy a group demand (by sanctioning the teacher) before it becomes public and places the school system within the context of a community conflict. Furthermore, both administrators and teachers might anticipate adverse response and, hence, modify their behavior before a demand is made explicit.

Parents, perhaps, are a more potent source of external pressure. The potential for conflict between parent and teacher is substantial because of incompatible claims of each for authority over the child. Parents are likely to be hostile toward an educational system which threatens to socialize their children away from the values dominant within the family. The majority of a sample of Oregon residents voiced this concern. Corroborating the Oregon findings, Jennings

(1966:18) reported that the substance of parental complaints lies in the domain of religion and politics. He suggests that, "Instruction in the school—no matter how oblique—which threatens to undermine these orientations may be viewed very dimly by parents jealous of this prerogative. Even teaching about presumably objective facts, to say nothing of calling for tolerance of nonconformity or outright pitches for a point of view, may be enough to elicit a grievance. . . ." On the other hand, there was no clear direction to the complaints; parents about as frequently felt the content of a course was too conservative as too liberal.

Thus, parental pressure cannot be used to explain the status quo orientation of the social studies curriculum. Furthermore, many of the parents who were disturbed did nothing about it. Only 19 percent of those parents who were upset by what a child was taught contacted the school in order to seek a redress of grievances. Again, one genuine hell-raising parent can have an influence beyond what is indicated by this percentage. The point is that in the normal, day-to-day operation of the schools, external demands are a less important source of constraint than are internal (especially administrative) expectations. Even when action against the school is initiated, it is rare that the strategy of influence will be an organizational effort. Organizational participation, probably signifying that a particular grievance has surfaced into a public issue, occurs in about 10 percent of the cases of attempted influence that Jennings discovered.

SCHOOLS AS MIRROR IMAGES

The idea of the school as the mirror image of the society certainly is compatible with the argument of this paper. Lacking values in conflict with those dominant in the community, schools hardly can be expected to act as agents of change. Yet the evidence for this conclusion is less than satisfying. Some sparse evidence, such as the work of Litt (1963) and Pock (1967) suggests that the values typical of a school's personnel seem to be comparable to values presumed to be typical of a particular type of community; for example, schools in upper income areas have teachers and students with more liberal values and offer more realistic social studies curricula than schools in other areas.

The basic problem with this argument is that no explanation has been offered for the fact that the personnel within a school do not necessarily have social class characteristics similar to those dominant in the community. Moreover, such arguments assume that social classes have clearly discernible values which are more or less automatically translated into an educational philosophy. The fact that most of the early work in school-community relations was done by sociologists probably contributed to the conclusion that classes and values could be roughly equated. However, this line of research neglected the role of occupational socialization in the organization of attitudes. While it certainly is true that teachers and administrators are "middle class," they are products of a unique recruitment process which makes it likely that they will exaggerate, rather than merely reflect, a stereotypic middle class set of values. The role of the community, however this role is made manifest, is to set margins within which the educational task is to be performed. It is only upon the relatively rare occasions when the margins are breached that conflict between the school and community erupts. As Charters (1953: 282) notes:

It is possible that something which we shall call a "margin of tolerance" describes the school-community relationship. Citizens of each community may delegate to school personnel the freedom to educate youth according to their professional consciences—but freedom within a certain well defined (or ill-defined) bounds. The boundary is composed of values dear to the particular community. If school personnel over-step the boundary, crisis ensues and community values enter the determination of school affairs.

INTERNAL STRUCTURE

According to the above interpretation, we should look more closely at the internal structure of the school system to find out why it operates in defense of the status quo. If, as we can probably assume, administrators would prefer to keep community values out of the determination of school affairs, they must make certain that the margin of tolerance is not approached. In order to do this, they need to recruit teachers whose conduct is likely to cause little trouble. In short, the key to understanding why education is so admirably suited for its task is the recruitment process. The recruitment process in public education should be understood within the context of the educational "establishment." The word "establishment," which has been ridiculed when applied to the general political system, seems quite apt when considering the educational subsystem. Teacher training programs, through which teachers must pass in order to be certified, provide the manpower. Schools of education are more closely coordinated than are most academic departments. They have become part of a stable pattern of interactions with accrediting associations, state departments of education, professional associations of teachers, and administrative associations. Certainly the most powerful force within the establishment is the school of education; but this power is reinforced by the support of the other components of the establishment. The crucial determinant of the existence, or lack thereof, of an establishment is a value consensus. Without having the evidence which would make such an assertion beyond question, it seems to us that there is substantial agreement among professional educators concerning the appropriate role of controversy in the classroom and the expected behavior of teachers. The point may be disputed, but the low level of tolerance within the establishment seems to operate in the direction of driving out the dissenters.

Schools of education are very poor. Academically, the faculty of education schools ranks near the bottom. Attitudinally, the faculty of education schools appears more conservative and authoritarian than the faculties of other academic disciplines. Consequently, students attracted to education generally are the least capable on the college campus; they tend to be somewhat more conservative than the norm. Given the quality of education and the type of student recruited, it is not surprising that the products of schools of education do not view the classroom as an opportunity to develop creative thinking on the part of students. For instance, Jennings and Zeigler (1970), using an index of expressivism, found that 19 percent of the social studies teachers with education majors in college as compared with 55 percent of those with majors in social sciences were highly expressive.

Occupational socialization operates to reinforce the biases introduced in teacher training (Guba, et al., 1959:274–275). The longer one teaches, the less likely the possibility of engaging in risk taking behavior; the longer one teaches, the more custodial becomes one's approach to the classroom. The goals of education gradually become dominated by concern with control of behavior, creation of respect for authority, and establishment of orderly behavior. Recently we have seen, in the current determination of schools to establish dress regulations for students, the extent to which such concerns are significant. Teachers, in insisting upon their authority over students, readily acquiesce to administrators' power over them. Corwin, for instance, noted that teachers accept the legitimacy of administrative decision-making even in the area of classroom performance. In the authority system of the schools there is a place for everybody; in order to succeed it is merely necessary that one avoid trying to move up. Thus Jennings and Zeigler (1969) found a strong association between administrator's approval and acquiescent teacher behavior.

The recent disturbances in public education—teacher strikes and student unrest—can be understood as attempts to move up in the structure of authority. Consequently, administrators resist teacher demands and teachers resist student demands. In neither case has the making of demands escalated to the point of seriously threatening the established order. In both cases the responses to demands for restructuring have been repressive (see Rosenthal, 1969:96–109).

If we accept the argument that a conservative establishment is the major influence upon educational decision-making, then the participation of competitive units in the decision-making process becomes crucial. Generally, as we have argued, the school and the community interact only in cases of margin violation. In the normal decision-making process, the school board has a greater opportunity to compete with the administration for the control of educational policy. Generally it has been assumed that because school board members are recruited from the dominant class within a community, this body operates to reinforce commitment to the status quo. This assumption, however, is not supported by the available evidence.

Since all political bodies are dominated by those with the time and money to engage in politics, why should the school board— merely because it is typical of the political recruitment process— operate to maintain the status quo any more than other political institutions? Actually, the classes from which school board membership is drawn tend to be among the more liberal and tolerant within the community. Further, school board members have not endured the crippling *professional* socialization of the educational establishment.

Therefore, it is possible that school boards—to the extent that they can resist the strong pressure of cooptation from the administration—can serve as agents of change within the educational system. Such an assertion is supported by the recent research of Crain (1968). He found that school superintendents were likely to resist demands for desegregation but that, when the power to make decisions was taken from the superintendent by the school board, progress toward desegregation was more likely to occur. Likewise, Rosenthal (1969:143–153) reported that school boards in the cities he studied (with but one exception) tended to take the lead in establishing policies relating to integration.

The initiative that school boards have exhibited with respect to integration policies well may prove to be an issue-specific phenomenon rather than an indicator of a general trend. It may be the case that changes in school integration policies are inevitable and that board-inspired innovation merely is an example of short run marginal adjustment. Or, it may be that the nature of the integration issue is such that the school board—inasmuch as it is a lay institution which is roughly representative of non-professional values— is the only agent of the educational system which is competent to deal with it. Integration has much broader ramifications and attracts much wider attention than other issues confronting education. Perhaps it is "too hot" or too political an issue for professional administrators (whose expertise and resources do not extend to such matters) to handle.

Wherever the truth of the matter lies, the fact remains that in this one issue area, lay boards *have* exerted themselves, and they *have* established policy independent of the more conservative and "professional" organs of the educational establishment. It remains to be seen whether the momentum thus generated will lead them into other areas of involvement in which professional resources are more apparent and, if so, whether they will be able to withstand the pressures imposed by their respective administrations. These pressures— to resist intrusion into technical matters—might be less irresistible if the scope of conflict is enlarged. In conditions of expanded conflict, the resources of non-professionals are potentially greater. Viewed from this perspective, the characteristic style of the educational establishment (the minimization of conflict) is rational because there is a higher value placed upon technical resources. We would argue, however, that at this particular juncture in the development of the nation, the social consequences of technical expertise are too costly.

REFERENCES

ALMOND, GABRIEL, AND SIDNEY VERBA, *The Civic Culture.* Princeton: Princeton University Press, 1963.

BROWN, STUART GERRY, AND CHARLES L. PELTHIER, *Government in Our Republic* (revised edition). New York: Macmillan, 1964.

CHARTERS, W. W., JR., "Social Class Analysis and the Control of Public Education." *Harvard Educational Review,* 23 (Fall, 1953): 268–283. [Included as Chapter 6 in this volume.—Eds.]

COLE, WILLIAM E., AND CHARLES S. MONTGOMERY, *High School Sociology.* Boston: Allyn and Bacon, 1963.

CRAIN, ROBERT L., *The Politics of School Desegregation.* Chicago: Aldine, 1968.

GIRAULT, EMILY S., "Psychology and Sociology." Pp. 218–237 in C. Benjamin Cox and Byron G. Massialas (eds.), *Social Studies in the United States.* New York: Harcourt, Brace and World, 1967.

GUBA, EGON G., PHILIP W. JACKSON, AND CHARLES E. BIDWELL, "Occupational Choice and the Teaching Career." *Educational Research Bulletin,*

38 (1959): 1–12. Reprinted in W. W. Charters and N. L. Gage (eds.), *Readings in the Social Psychology of Education.* Boston: Allyn and Bacon, 1963.

HENRY, JULES, "Attitude Organization in Elementary School Classrooms." *American Journal of Orthopsychiatry,* 27 (1957): 117–133.

HUNT, MAURICE P., AND LAWRENCE E. METCALF, *Teaching High School Social Studies: Problems in Reflective Thinking and Social Understanding.* New York: Harper and Row, 1943.

JENNINGS, M. KENT, "Parental Grievances and School Politics." Paper presented at the CASEA Conference on Politics and Education, University of Oregon, Eugene, Oregon, 1966.

JENNINGS, M. KENT, AND RICHARD G. NIEMI, "The Transmission of Political Values from Parent to Child." *American Political Science Review,* 62 (March, 1968): 169–84.

JENNINGS, M. KENT, AND L. HARMON ZEIGLER, "The Politics of Teacher-Administrator Relations." *Education and Social Science,* 1 (1969): 73–82.

———, "Political Expressivism Among High School Teachers." In Roberta Siegel (ed.), *Learning About Politics.* New York: Random House, 1970.

LITT, EDGAR, "Civic Education, Community Norms, and Political Indoctrination." *American Sociological Review,* 28 (February, 1963): 69–75.

LUDLUM, ROBERT P., et al., *American Government.* Boston: Houghton Mifflin, 1965.

MASSIALAS, BYRON G., "American Government: We Are the Greatest!" Pp. 167–95 in C. Benjamin Cox and Byron G. Massialas (eds.), *Social Studies in the United States.* New York: Harcourt, Brace and World, 1967.

McCLENOGHAN, WILLIAM A., *Magruder's American Government.* Boston: Allyn and Bacon, 1966.

POCK, JOHN C., *Attitudes Toward Civil Liberties Among High School Seniors.* Washington, D.C.: U. S. Department of Health, Education, and Welfare. Cooperative Research Project No. 5-8167, 1967.

ROSENTHAL, ALAN, *Pedagogues and Power: Teacher Groups in School Politics.* Syracuse: Syracuse University Press, 1969.

WEISER, JOHN C., AND JAMES E. HAYES, "Democratic Attitudes of Teachers and Prospective Teachers." *Phi Delta Kappan,* 47 (May, 1966): 476–81.

ZEIGLER, L. HARMON, *The Political Life of American Teachers.* Englewood Cliffs, N.J.: Prentice-Hall, 1967.

chapter three

Teachers' organizations:
The new militancy

MYRON BRENTON

NEA* headquarters is located in an $11,000,000, Washington-modern edifice all its own, a brisk five-minute walk from the White House. It houses 34 departments (like audiovisual instruction, elementary school principals, etc.), 18 headquarters divisions (educational technology, research, radio and television, etc.), 25 commissions (budget, credentials, educational television, etc.), and an elaborate internal decision-making structure to encompass the needs and wishes of its 59 state and more than 8,000 local affiliated associations. Theoretically, policy is set by the 7,000 delegates to the Representative Assembly, which meets annually. Practically, the executive committee receiving direction from the powerful state associations, has much to do with the shaping of policy. The ordinary classroom teacher, remote from the sources of power, tends to find himself in as much of a bureaucracy in the NEA as in his school district.

NEA's membership in 1968 was past the million mark, including teachers and administrators. In terms of its potential power, it peaked several years earlier, however, at a little over 50 percent of the nation's teachers. This has become a troublesome fact of life for the organization, which keeps pushing hard for new members. In conjunction with its affiliates, though, the NEA affects the welfare of more than 1,750,000 teachers. Its 1968 budget was over $15,-000,000.

The NEA has had a considerable share in raising the standards

* [National Education Association—Ed.]

of the teaching field and upgrading education in the United States. (In recent years its National Commission on Teacher Education and Professional Standards [NCTEPS] has been especially active in this area.) The NEA has helped bring to fruition several major federal aid to education bills, particularly when it reversed its traditional stand against federal support for private and parochial schools. Along with the AFT [American Federation of Teachers], it called for federal aid long before it became popular to do so; then, as now, extreme right-wing groups accused it of being Communist.

But for the most part during its history the NEA has shied away from controversy and was often more facile with slogans about quality education than with action to bring this about. Until the past few years the NEA was dominated by administrators, even though the majority of its members are classroom teachers. The image it gained was of a stodgy, status quo-oriented establishment institution, one it's trying to live down. In its earlier years, in fact, as a recent historical account has it, the NEA was more of an instrument for controlling teachers than for helping them.[1] Furthermore, one of its major thrusts has been expansionist; it has been a major player of the membership numbers game. Though the practice has been waning the past few years, administrators in school districts all over the country coerced teachers into joining the NEA. Applicants for teaching positions were handed NEA membership blanks along with employment application forms, or were otherwise pressured into signing up. In the eyes of the administrators, membership in the NEA and its affiliates was equated with "professionalism"—while the teacher who didn't want to join or, worse, joined the teacher's union, was looked upon askance.

All in all, the NEA's impact overall, legislatively and otherwise, is far from commensurate with its prodigious expenditures of time, energy, and money. This is so despite the fact that during the Eisenhower regime the NEA had the reputation of practically running USOE [U.S. Office of Education]. The then-Secretary of Health, Education and Welfare, Arthur S. Flemming, had the habit of phoning NEA headquarters from his limousines to report on important legislative matters.) In recent years the NEA has lost considerable power and influence to a coalition of tough-minded, change-oriented men from the foundations, from the upper echelons of a newly powerful USOE, and from elsewhere.[2]

[1] Laurence Iannaccone, *Politics in Education* (New York, The Center for Applied Research in Education, 1967), Ch. 2.

[2] For an excellent brief account of NEA's history, see Peter Janssen, "NEA: The Reluctant Dragon," *Saturday Review* (June 17, 1967).

Though it has always operated under the credo of "one big happy educational family," the past decade has seen members of that family increasingly at one another's [throats]. Much of the dissent has come from angry, impatient, urban-centered young teacher-leaders of their local NEA affiliates. They no more liked the idea of being paternalized and dominated within the NEA than within the schools. Nor did they like the spectacle of a brash, aggressive AFT grabbing off such plums as New York City (whose ninety-odd NEA affiliates it whipped into a union in 1960), Chicago, Boston, Washington, D.C. (in the NEA's own backyard), and other major cities. And those angry young men had considerable distaste for the conservatism of NEA's administrator-leaders, who had come from small towns or rural areas and had little feeling or concern for city problems. Many of its powerful state affiliates still are conservative and administrator-dominated. Thus, NEA's civil rights record was, until recently, poor: It avoided taking a stand on school desegregation until the Supreme Court decision of 1954. It had no cabinet-level Negroes in its hierarchy nor did it elect a Negro president until 1968, and the last of its white and black separate Southern affiliates were to be merged (with considerable pressure from the NEA) in 1969. It wasn't until 1968, in fact, that the NEA organized a task force to deal with urban school problems and a human relations center to deal with the human rights of students and teachers; previously it attacked such problems in piecemeal fashion. But the NEA has fought hard for the rights of Negro teachers dismissed from Southern school districts in the wake of desegregation, and has contributed substantial sums to help them.

The past decade, then, has seen an intensive amount of infighting within the NEA, and the balance of power has been shifting from administrators to teachers. Squeezed by AFT victories on the one hand, and the demands of its own aggressive teachers on the other, in 1967 the NEA reversed an historic stand against strikes and passed a resolution okaying work stoppages as a last resort. (Prior to that time its ultimate weapon was "sanctions"—blackballing a district by warning teachers not to take jobs there.) By 1969 the school superintendents had become so affronted by teacher power that the relationship between their group, the American Association of School Administrators, and the NEA, was organizationally very tenuous. And power fights were being played out among other conservative, moderate, and militant factions in the NEA family.

The AFT, too—160,000 strong and, despite its puny size, in control of some of the biggest cities—is far from running a harmonious shop these days. Traditionally allied with American labor's liberal wing, it has concentrated on teacher welfare and also been strong on academic freedom and civil rights. Its civil rights record has, until recently, been a much better one than the NEA's. It backed school desegregation years before the 1954 Supreme Court decision, ran freedom schools for Southern Negro students and desegregated or suspended its own few Southern locals. But as salaries and working conditions have improved, its members have become more protectionist-minded. A number of locals, for instance, have veto power over transfer of teachers to ghetto schools, preventing the integration of faculties and overloading those schools with inexperienced teachers.

Despite the fact that his union was strongly identified as alienated from the low-income communities, Albert Shanker, president of the UFT [United Federation of Teachers], became the top vote-getter of the twenty persons elected to vice-presidencies at the AFT's 1968 convention. Disenchanted with the outcome of this convention, which also saw Shanker successfully weaken a strong community control resolution, dissidents promptly formed a new caucus.

The UFT is the foremost example of a formerly progressive teachers' union grown increasingly powerful, political, and protectionist. In the early 1960's it backed a school boycott, the pairing of schools and the reorganization of the middle grades—all to promote integration. It gave substantial sums to support civil rights demonstrations in Selma, Alabama, and urged its members to vote for a civilian review board to hear cases of police brutality. But from the mid-1960's on, things changed. Ghetto militants became more vocal in denouncing the failure of the schools to educate their children, and some accused teachers of incompetence. They were outraged by the union's consistent refusal to bend on the transfer issue. Many teachers themselves reflect the general bias against nonwhites, as recent studies indicate. The union refused to back a second boycott of the schools. With the establishment of community control demonstration centers at IS 201 in Harlem (followed by two more, in Brooklyn's Ocean Hill-Brownsville slum and in lower Manhattan) repeated clashes between the union and the black community occurred in 1966 and 1967. Clashes would probably have come anyway, but they were more frequent and intense because the Board of Education's professionals—hostile to the idea of community control—hadn't given the demonstration districts clear guidelines as to their powers.

At any rate, black teachers began to break away from the UFT. Many of the whites were unable to empathize with the black community's efforts to better its schools; all they could see were threats:

growing black militancy, more violence in the schools, intrusion into professional matters (there were demands that district superintendents be locally elected and teachers evaluated by the community), the irrational fear that people were literally going to invade their classrooms and tell them how to teach.

Late 1966 to early 1968 saw a continual series of confrontations between the UFT and IS 201, the latter also having plenty of problems getting Board of Education cooperation for even the most trifling matters. In the fall of 1967 the UFT struck the city for three weeks over issues that left many teachers frankly confused. One action that preceded the strike—an inflammatory "disruptive child" clause the union wanted inserted in the new contract, giving teachers the right to summarily remove any child from class—bitterly offended the black communities. Their schools remained open during the strike, which was ostensibly called to force the Board of Education to expand the UFT's More Effective Schools program. A lot of rank-and-file teachers, however, thought they were staying out to get a better pay package, as well. When the strike ended with no wage gains other than those already won, many teachers were furious. (Some observers saw the strike calculated to serve a few more subtle purposes: to defeat a new negotiations procedure the city was attempting to set up, and to show the troublesome demonstration districts a little teacher muscle.) Then Shanker was jailed for having violated the states's anti-strike law and the anger of rank-and-filers understandably melted. As one union official unofficially put it, "Even teachers who felt he'd let them down now backed him. He became a martyr."

Throughout the whole of 1968 there were ugly clashes between white teachers and people in the ghetto areas, the main focal point now being the Ocean Hill-Brownsville community control district. (Of earlier incidents, commented sociologist David Rogers in a study of New York City's school bureaucracy, "It is unfortunate that teachers and parents, who are both victims of the school system, should become so involved in power seeking that they take it out on one another." [3]) At one point the UFT struck the district to protect teachers the district didn't find acceptable. It lobbied heavily and expensively in Albany, the state capital, whose lawmakers were considering bills to decentralize all of New York City's cumbersome school system, being rewarded with the passage of a very weak decentralization bill.

By fall of 1968 the confrontation had focused dangerously on

[3] David Rogers, *110 Livingston Street* (New York, Random House, 1968), p. 199.

nineteen teachers the district claimed were sabotaging community control efforts. Ocean Hill-Brownsville's governing board dismissed them from the district and ordered them to report to central headquarters for reassignment. Charging that the teachers had been "fired," claiming due process violations with respect to involuntary transfers, and brandishing "mob rule" signs (which the black community saw as racist code words), the UFT struck. It didn't strike alone. It formed a solid alliance with the Council of Supervisory Associations, a highly conservative body of school administrators that had fought almost every desegregation measure the union in calmer days had supported. The UFT-CSA alliance notably shifted educational politics in New York City. The alliance came about because the CSA was even more fearful of community control than the UFT was: The ghetto communities, tired of being educational colonies, were demanding the right to bypass the city's so-called merit list of (white) principals and to choose their own black and Puerto Rican administrators.

Fifty thousand teachers (out of about 55,000) stayed out of school, along with the administrators and—a couple of weeks later—the custodians, who shut off boilers and changed door locks in an effort to keep nonstriking teachers, parents and students from entering locked schools. A few schools were forced open and kept open, though most white parents supported the UFT. Thus, more than 1,000,000 schoolchildren were deprived of a month of school. The disturbances gave the UFT ammunition with which to demonstrate to Albany lawmakers that community control (or meaningful decentralization) wasn't viable in New York City. The union had a number of concerns. It couldn't afford to lose its hard-fought right to bargain on a city-wide basis. It wanted no part of any decentralization scheme that would allow thirty-odd local boards to hire, fire, and transfer teachers. It was also worried about its dwindling membership in the demonstration districts: Few of the teachers who volunteered to teach there—though largely white and Jewish, just like the bulk of loyal UFT teachers—signed up. (Before the end of the strike the union sought to gain an "agency shop," which would have had nonunion teachers paying dues, as a price for settlement.) For their part, the community control districts had some compelling interests of their own—most importantly, to consolidate and build on their very tenuous power base.

Aroused by the union leadership, rank-and-file teachers were genuinely frightened by the prospect of community control, or even decentralization. The actions of a few black extremists and rising anti-Semitism in the black areas of the city didn't help matters. Dur-

ing the strike some anti-Semitic leaflets were stuffed in teachers'
mailboxes in a few ghetto schools; the union reproduced these by
the thousands and the city was flooded with them, making the threat
of anti-Semitism loom much larger than it was. By this time the city
was polarized, mostly along racial lines. It became increasingly clear
that the UFT was out to kill decentralization. The complexities and
virulence surrounding the strike were exacerbated by the failure of
the Board of Education, Mayor John V. Lindsay, and the Ford
Foundation, which financed the demonstration districts, to provide
effective leadership.

The strike ended on November 17 with a complicated agreement
that put observers into the Ocean Hill-Brownsville schools, established a state trusteeship over the district, and gave the union right
to full grievance procedures in the case of involuntary transfers.
The agreement also added forty-five minutes to the school day,
eliminated holidays, and shortened vacations—ostensibly to help
students make up instructional time, but in fact as a thinly veiled
mechanism for allowing teachers to make up pay lost during the
strike. The makeup time brought more tensions: It prompted high
school students to demonstrate and was a factor in fresh disturbances surrounding UFT teachers, this time back at the IS 201 district. These occurred precisely when lawmakers in Albany were getting ready to vote on new school decentralization measures, and
Shanker warned of the possibility of new city-wide strikes.

The UFT lobbied heavily in Albany, as before, and also spent
much time, money, and energy attempting to defeat local politicians, up for reelections, who had been strong for community control. It found itself in the ironic position of backing lawmakers
hostile to community control but who had voted for strong anti-
strike laws directed at public employees. In Albany a very weak
decentralization bill was passed—one that also gave the union what
it had wanted right along, the elimination of the three decentral-
ized districts. During the strike the UFT had dismissed a vice-presi-
dent from its hierarchy, one who was publicly protesting its policies.
Now many remaining dissident UFT members quietly dropped out,
and organizational changes made it very difficult—or next to impossible—for those who remained to protest union policy with any
kind of effectiveness. The new decentralization bill considerably
strengthening its members' rights, internal opponents melting away,
the UFT emerged more powerful than ever.

Presently, the NEA and AFT are locked in bitter jurisdictional
battles that cost them heavily in money and talent, both of which
could obviously be put to more constructive use on behalf of edu-

cation. (In Michigan alone, according to one informant, both sides spent around $200,000.) There's good reason to believe a merger between the two organizations will at some time, possibly by 1975, take place. Merger talk has been in the air for years, both overtly (the AFT periodically makes a grandstanding offer, via the press, for an NEA-AFT merger) and covertly (secret talks between members of both groups are held from time to time). Major obstacles to merger are said to be NEA's administrators and the AFT's union affiliation. As the distinctions between the two organizations keep blurring, these obstacles may well disappear. How power would be divided may prove a bigger problem in the long run. At any rate, there are signs that mergers between locals in various states will precede a national merger.

Such a merger would create one powerful educational monolith —a teacher's organization with the ability to shut down most or all of the nation's schools at once. It's not the most comfortable prospect to contemplate. "It may be necessary to have a nationwide stoppage," David Selden, AFT president, has said, "to bring about a reallocation of resources for the schools."

Whether or not that possibility is a remote one, some implications of growing teacher power bear considering. The fact of the matter is, most teachers aren't committed to their careers or their professional organizations. Housewives and housewives-to-be, or men who run from school to a second job, may work hard and may work well —but they have little interest in what goes on beyond their classrooms. "Teaching is just a job," admitted a teacher, the mother of three, who perhaps typifies the attitude of many women in the field. "I began to teach because I enjoy working with children, because I didn't like to come home in the rush hour . . . It's a job that's very convenient for me as a mother. My hours are excellent. My pay is good. Maybe I'm a little better educated than a lot of women. Maybe I put a little more into my work. But it's still just a job." Such people aren't very active, inquiring members of their profession. *The Political Life of American Teachers* shows that teachers join their organizations because they think they'll be helped professionally and intellectually, because they're asked to or expected to, or because they can "increase their political power" by having the teachers' group "lobby for them and, if necessary, defend them against community attack." Most teachers join for the first or second reasons. Only about 15 percent are active in their organizations in the sense of giving much time and effort to them.[4]

[4] Harmon Zeigler, *The Political Life of American Teachers* (Englewood Cliffs, N.J., Prentice-Hall, Inc., 1967), p. 61.

Teachers have turned to the NEA or AFT and their affiliates in large numbers because, lacking the former deep identification with school and community, they can identify with their group, and be helped by it. But that doesn't necessarily mean they're any closer to the sources of power—to the "front office" so to speak—of their organizations than they are to the power sources of the school or community. It doesn't even mean they're interested in being close to it. All this has considerable import as teachers' organizations grow stronger, more militant, more political, and demand an increasing voice in educational decision making.

What's good for teacher may be good for education, and then again, may be in fundamental contradiction with it. It only muddies the waters to say, as teacher-leaders sometimes do, that everything benefiting teacher benefits students—especially when some teacher groups now come to the conference table with a couple of hundred contractual demands, most of which can be narrowly defined as welfare items. As for strikes, they may revolve in straightforward fashion around the surface issues, and then again they may have underlying political significance whose ramifications go far beyond. Issues of which the rank-and-file may be as unaware as the general public. None of this is to suggest that teachers shouldn't ask for more power or be denied the right to strike. But teachers can be cogs in their organizational machine as in any other. In teachers' healthy quest for greater autonomy, for the right to run their own show, this is the danger.

chapter four

State politics of education

FREDERICK M. WIRT AND MICHAEL W. KIRST

Although popular folklore conceives of schools as locally controlled, the state has taken a hand in them for many decades. Indeed, by 1970 as we have seen, it is highly questionable how much local control is a reality. But the components of that political authority termed the *state* need further specification. For such authority is partly formal, a matter of state constitutional requirements and state officers, and partly informal, a matter of pressure groups and current values. Given the variety of American federalism discussed earlier and its accompanying individualism, there should be differences in these political authorities and hence in these conversion processes. It may be that such diverse political cultures can operate to fend off the nationalizing trends noted earlier. In that case, the values of a diverse localism, deposited from our past, still give some reality to the notion of local control.

GROWTH OF THE STATE ROLE
IN LOCAL SCHOOLS [1]

Most state constitutions make local education a legal responsibility of the state. The United States Constitution is silent with regard to education; consequently, education is a reserved power of

"State Politics of Education" (editors' title). From Frederick M. Wirt and Michael W. Kirst, *The Political Web of American Schools* (Boston: Little, Brown and Company, 1972), pp. 111–12; 114–24. Copyright © 1972 by Little, Brown and Company (Inc.). Reprinted by permission of the publisher and the authors.

[1] For an overview of state organization for education see Edgar L. Morphet and David Jesser, *Emerging State Responsibilities for Education* (Denver: Improving State Leadership in Education, 1970). For encyclopedic detail on the states' role in developing and shaping local schools' organization and power, see Edgar Fuller and Jim B. Pearson (eds.), *Education in the States*, 2 vols. (Washington, D.C.: NEA, 1969).

the states. These three levels of educational government interact on policies, but only state statutes stipulate in detail how schools are to be governed. In effect, although much control is delegated to district boards, the states vary considerably in the independence of those boards from the state.

The contemporary arrangement differs sharply from that existing at the nation's opening, for there was no state school administration then. Early school laws of the American colonies stemmed from the state legislature and other organs of general government making education policy directly. Schools were small, with unspecialized curricula, and the state role was to "protect and encourage" schools rather than financially support them. Thus there were no state boards of education or chief state school officers. By 1820, however, thirteen of the twenty states had developed constitutional provisions for education. The position of chief state school officer (CSSO) had emerged in some states in 1836, and by 1870 most states provided for them; state boards of education appeared about the same time. A number of the early CSSO's played a crucial role in leading public opinion to support public education.

From these early beginnings, state involvement in local schools has expanded both in programs and personnel. Over time, several important decisions have come to be made at the state level. Most states *define the program scope,* such as kindergarten, vocational education, or junior college.[2] The legislature usually delegates to the state board of education the prerogative to *set minimum standards* for curriculum, pupil promotion and graduation, and even instructional materials. Some state boards *adopt a standard course of study* or detailed guidelines for subject areas such as civics or math. Southern states in particular *adopt textbooks* that are distributed to all public schools. State regulations and statutes are even more detailed with respect to requirements for *certification of teachers.* Most states stipulate the length of the training program, define some specifics on its content, and accredit training institutions.

The most visible state political issue has been financial support for education. Some states set tax limits for local districts and require certain local budget breakdowns. A state property equalization board can be a crucial factor in providing for adjustments in local property assessment practices.[3] In all of these areas, however, policies among states vary enormously. . . .

[2] See Michael D. Usdan, David Minar, and Emanuel Hurwitz, *Education and State Politics* (New York: Teachers College Press, Columbia University, 1969).

[3] For an overview of the processes and programs of state finance, see Charles Benson, *Economics of Public Education* (Boston: Houghton Mifflin, 1967); and

Generally speaking, the state role has focused on establishing minimum standards in education while encouraging local districts to exceed them. This role stems from one aspect of American egalitarianism, the belief that the general welfare requires a floor for educational opportunity.[4] State employees must inspect local districts to ensure that this floor is provided through certain courses, minimum school attendance or minimum tax levies. To encourage local initiative, most states provide tax leeway for local districts that want to exceed state minimums, e.g., matching incentive payments for districts whose tax rate exceeds the state minimum.

This state role arises from another consideration, the pull of localism. The evolution of state influence on and financial support for local schools has been replete with philosophical and practical political struggles between state and local jurisdictions. The constitutional power of state government has been in constant tension with a widely held value that the soundest educational policy is determined locally. "Local control" has become a powerful and pervasive political shibboleth, in many states restricting the financial and leadership support of state agencies. A study of the Northeast concluded that "the most pervasive and persistent of depressants on state school subsidies is rural localism."[5] We shall return to this issue subsequently but move now to a fuller review of state school political authorities.

THE AUTHORITATIVE STATE POLITICAL SYSTEM

GOVERNORS AND LEGISLATORS

One area of historic controversy has been whether educational policy should be in the effective control of the governor, a separate board or boards, the legislature, a commissioner, or a combination of these. Almost every state has had its peculiar battles about this question. However, the legacy of "no politics in education" has

---

Dick Netzer, *Economics of the Property Tax* (Washington, D.C.: Brookings Institution, 1966).

[4] For a critique of financial minimums and state aid formulas, see James Guthrie et al., *Schools and Inequality* (Cambridge: MIT Press, 1971). A listing of required courses for each state, illustrating the minimums, can be found in George D. Marconnit, "State Legislatures and the School Curriculum," *Phi Delta Kappan,* 49 (1968), 269–72.

[5] Stephen K. Bailey et al., *Schoolmen and Politics* (Syracuse: Syracuse University Press, 1962), 47.

helped to shape the outcome of this question, often ending in restricting the influence of elected officials such as the governor and legislature.

For instance, when in 1784 the New York State Board of Regents was established to formulate educational policies for the state, the governor was very powerful. Key politicians, however, had a central role in appointing and managing the board, often composed of legislators and big city mayors. After only three years, however, a new act reduced the control of these leaders, and the regents became a fourth branch of government—independent of governor, legislature, and even court. Bailey and his associates concluded:

> What is true of the New York State Board of Regents is true to a lesser degree of the other state boards of education in the Northeast. Although in the other seven states, appointment to the boards is made by the governor (often with legislative consent) rather than by the legislature alone, the effective independence of the boards from direct political pressure and from the political rhythms of gubernatorial and legislative elections is a long standing tradition.[6]

Any proposals to reduce this political independence in New England has brought resistance from professional schoolmen, because it would "inevitably plunge educational leadership and the schools into a maelstrom of partisan politics to the detriment of all concerned." [7]

The governors and the legislatures, however, maintain control of state financial-aid legislation. Issues of educational finance inevitably involve judgments on educational programs and priorities, so the constitutional separation of education from general state government can never extend to many important educational issues. Indeed, in most if not all states, public education is the largest single state budget item, and politicians, of course, know that the electorate responds to tax increases. Money is obviously a basic resource, and the amounts available for education are so large as to attract considerable political attention. As close analysts of governmental costs have noted:

> More public funds are expended for education [1964] than for any other domestic service of government, and this has been true consistently through-

⁶ Ibid., 8.
⁷ Clyde B. Moore, *Educational Growth and the New York State Constitution* (Albany: New York State Educational Conference Board, February, 1958), as cited in Bailey, 9.

out this century and probably for a considerable time before that. In fact, until World War II, the peacetime costs of education substantially exceeded those for national defense.[8]

The weight of such monies gives much power to those who dispose it, and in the states these are the governor and legislature. Any governor is a hard man to fight when he wants to hold the line on state finance. Appropriation committees in the legislature are also watchdogs for the state treasury, ranking at the top of all committees in seniority, prestige, and power. In any given year, however, tight budget constraints are rarely aimed at education alone but extend across all state government functions.[9]

Enormous differences exist among states in the scope of gubernatorial and legislative concern with and expertise in education. Thus, in California, the legislature, which has a large, full-time staff for its education committee, between 1961 and 1967 passed bills in such areas as licensing of teachers, school resdistricting, the measurement of student achievement, and teaching of reading and foreign languages. Elsewhere, state legislators are part-timers, paid less than $5,000, and with no staff that has expertise in education policy. In some of these states, education legislation is confined to desegregation and routine financial aid. But in Texas, where education finance revision is the major state issue, 40 percent of the members of the House are serving their first term, obviously inexperienced in this issue's complexity. Such variations should not conceal some similarities among the states, however. Everywhere financial problems dominate legislators' perception of education, and everywhere the gap between demands and resources is hard to close.[10]

The evidence we now have suggests that state legislators find education not to be an issue that provides much political leverage or attracts many votes. For example, a study of three midwest states concluded, "Relatively few public school proposals entertained in

[8] Frederick C. Mosher and Orville F. Poland, *The Costs of American Governments: Facts, Trends, Myths* (New York: Dodd, Mead, 1964), 116. For evidence of the dominant weight of schools in state expenditures since 1902, see ibid., 43.

[9] See Nicholas Masters et al., *State Politics and Public Schools* (New York: Knopf, 1964).

[10] Governor's Committee on Public Education, *Public Education in Texas* (Austin: Texas Education Agency, 1969). For a comparative perceptual study, see Leroy Ferguson, "How State Legislators View the Problem of School Needs," in Robert C. Crew (ed.), *State Politics* (Belmont: Wadsworth, 1968), 481. For a close examination of California, see Paul Collins, "Legislative Influence and the Changing Relationships of the California Educational Associations, 1960–1969," unpublished Ph.D. dissertation, University of California, Berkeley, 1971.

the legislative halls of the three states studied result from general public pressures or from wave-like 'public' protests." [11] Legislators and governors may feel they should respond to and support regularly the professional education lobby, but they have not been forced by widespread citizen demands to develop a continuing insight into educational issues or to mount a consistent educational crusade. As we noted earlier, education interest groups have attempted to mute competition between their professional organizations and other competing interests for state dollars, thereby reducing the conflict level and the pressures over school funding.

The role of the governor in education has been restricted by the lack of expert staff in his office with a viewpoint independent from the state department of education. In some states the CSSO is a member of the governor's cabinet; in others he is a separately elected official. Some governors have no education specialist at all, and others operate with only a one- or two-man personal staff.[12] Experience in several states indicates a leadership role in education by one governor which is then not continued by his successor. In effect, some governors have wanted to establish their statewide reputation through leadership in public education, but their effectiveness (or lack of it) has caused the successor of either party to attempt leadership in another field in order to build a separate record and political image.

STATE BOARDS OF EDUCATION

The state board is primarily a legitimating agency for broad policies; it leaves administration to the state superintendent and state department. Again, we find tremendous differences among states. Some boards are elected, some appointed by the governor, and some are constituted *ex officio*. Their size ranges from three members to over twenty; some meet weekly and others quarterly. Again, the variety seen here reflects the mosaic of American federalism with its underlying individualistic notions of how to govern.

But regardless of how they are selected, Sroufe has shown that state board members comprise a singularly homogeneous popula-

[11] Masters et al., 265.

[12] There is no recent comparative state study of the governor's role and staff for education policy. For a discussion of the governor's office, see Coleman P. Ransone, Jr., *The Office of the Governor in the United States* (University, Ala.: University of Alabama Press, 1956); and Duane Lockhard, *The Politics of State and Local Government* (New York: Macmillan, 1969), ch. 13.

tion of professionals earning high incomes.[13] Forty-five percent have
served on local boards, and three-fourths have lived in no more than
two states. There appear to be two streams of activity that might
lead someone of high education and status to become a state board
member. One path is increasingly responsible experience at the local level, then moving on to some state study groups or special com-
missions, and finally elevation to the state board. The less common
route is to gain eminence within a non-educational sector and then
be "tapped" for the board. Sroufe found that at the time of selection, state board members do not seem to have highly specific educational goals or to be concerned about certain educational issues.
Indeed, over half the appointed board members reported that they
first considered the work of the board only when the governor asked
them to accept.[14] The influence of political party elements in securing appointment is considerable, despite the nonpartisan myth surrounding much of education. Table 1 reveals this when it presents
the views of state school board members about the persons considered most influential in nominating candidates to the state board.

As for the alternative selection method, elections, these can be
accurately described as non-events; about half of the elected re-

TABLE 1   THE INFLUENTIALS IN NOMINATING CANDIDATES TO THE STATE BOARD OF EDUCATION

Influentials	Percentage of Respondents Assigning First Rank
Political party member, outside the legislature	30
Members of the legislature	19
Current board members	16
Chief state school officer	12
State education association	11
Governor's aids and advisors	3
Other school groups	2
Other (variety of noncombinable categories)	7

Source: Gerald E. Sroufe, "Recruitment Processes and Composition of State Boards of Education," paper presented at 1969 meeting of the American Educational Research Association.

[13] Gerald E. Sroufe, "Recruitment Processes and Composition of State Boards of Education," paper presented at 1969 meeting of the American Educational Research Association.
[14] In all but one of the states using the appointment model of selection, the governor is responsible for making the appointment.

spondents to a recent survey did not campaign at all. The typical candidate issues just one press release, so that public awareness and interest are minimal. The winner receives no pay, little publicity, and, not unsurprisingly, the position is rarely a political stepping stone. In short, elected members do not differ from appointed members, because, unlike most other statewide political contests, this election process is of low intensity.

This leads to Sroufe's speculation that the "reason board members are so much alike is that no one expects the board to be very influential in the formulation or implementation of state educational policy." [15] In fact, we know very little about the policy role of the state board, although it is clear that the electorate finds it exceedingly difficult to make substantive choices for membership to an unknown board. Popular disinterest is shown in the gap in total votes between this and other state offices in most elections. This would suggest that public demands for change in educational policies are probably transmitted more to elected political leaders and the state department of education rather than to the less-visible state board.

Functionally, the state board acts both as an implementing arm of the legislature and as a legislature in its own right. Indeed, its work covers the three traditional governing functions of legislating, administering, and adjudicating. Much of this arises because the discretion provided by the legislature is often quite wide.[16] For example, the legislature may set general requirements for administrative credentials but permit the state board to specify courses, experiences, and other requirements. Other customary functions of the state board are to act as court of appeals in disputes, define racial imbalance, create statewide testing, direct preparation of statewide syllabuses or courses, and oversee consolidation. Despite such authority, Koerner has concluded that the state board's potentially vast influence is used in only the most general way. "Either it allows the state department of education to make policies . . . or it yields a great deal of its power to local school authorities. Southern state boards are apt to be more domineering than northern, but all are permissive." [17]

The board's problem is that localism makes enforcement of its policies very difficult. Local districts can find ways to circumvent

[15] Sroufe, 22.

[16] James Koerner, *Who Controls American Education?* (Boston: Beacon Press, 1968), 85. The activities and influence of state boards of education is a dark continent in view of the paucity of research.

[17] Ibid.

the state because the board usually has no clear enforcement strategies. Further, state boards have little time or inclination to check
carefully on local compliance but must rely for staff work on the
state superintendent and his staff. Recommendations, analyses, and
outlining of alternatives are the responsibility of the state department civil servants and the CSSO. State boards rarely have their
own independent staffs but rather view the entire state department
as a resource to draw upon.[18]

STATE DEPARTMENTS OF EDUCATION

A reading of state constitutions and statutes would lead one to believe that the legislature and state board of education are the sole
sources for the authoritative allocation of values. The state department of education (SDE) is usually described as the executive or
implementing arm of the policy-making state board. Traditionally,
the SDE has close ties with the professional statewide associations
of teachers, administrators, curriculum specialists, etc., who provide
demands and supports for its decisions and recommendations to the
board. In fact, as we have seen, the SDE actually has broad areas of
policy making delegated to it by the state board, which then exercises minimal administrative oversight. Moreover, the state board
relies on the SDE to prepare its agenda and provide recommendations.

In effect, then, this state agency is the locus of a considerable
amount of authoritative allocation of values, whether in formulat-
ing specific regulations, allocating federal funds to local districts, or
executing the more detailed decisions of the state board. The administration and interpretation of the general and flexible man-
dates of the state board have a differential impact. Consequently,
because the values and actions of the SDE enhance the benefits of
some groups and individuals rather than others, we need to explore
its impact and orientation.[19]

How much influence the CSSO has depends on several factors—
primarily the strength and activism of the legislature, governor, and
state board.[20] Some state superintendents have dominated weak

[18] Many observations in this section have been drawn from a Ford Foundation
study of state distribution of federal aid, including consideration of state boards
in six states. See Joel S. Berke and Michael W. Kirst, *Federal Aid to Education:
Who Benefits? Who Governs?* (Lexington, Mass.: Heath, 1972).

[19] For the perceptions of local superintendents of SDE's, see Keith Goldhammer
et al., *Issues and Problems in Contemporary Educational Administration* (Eugene:
University of Oregon, 1967), ch. 4.

[20] See n. 18.

boards. Others have been limited severely by a strong legislature. Most superintendents find themselves somewhat constrained by the board and the legislature but have been able to exert a substantial, independent influence over state policy. Consequently, the CSSO and the staff of the SDE, through detailed regulations, actually write the final version of policies passed by the legislature and state board. The SDE's are less constrained by the state board and the legislature in the allocation of federal money funneled through the state. As we shall see, this federal money has given SDE's a greatly enhanced role in determining the content of local education programs and the priorities of intrastate financial allocation.[21]

The CSSO is almost always a member in good standing of the professional education fraternity. The pay and prestige of the office are low—lower than most big city superintendencies. His low pay depresses the salary range for his administrative officers and hinders recruitment of able and aggressive people. Despite these limits, SDE personnel have high responsibility and authority as the executive arm of the state board. Consequently, they are involved in such activities as teacher credentialing, technical assistance in subject areas, operation of agencies for handicapped children, and distribution of large amounts of state and federal aid. Conant's comment in 1964 about the political orientation of SDE's appears still true today.

The major weakness of all state departments of education I have encountered, with perhaps one or two exceptions, is that they are too much a part of the educational establishment. That is, I found many of these agencies . . . to be no more than "willing tools" of the interests and clientele, particularly the education association (that is, the state NEA affiliate). In more than one state I heard highly placed education and political officials claim that state departments of education "follow a party line" or reflect the public school mentality. . . . A grave shortcoming of our educational leadership at the state level, in my opinion, is often its unwillingness or incapacity to respond to forces outside the establishment. These agencies seldom solicit the opinions of educational experts or critics who are not associated with public schools or professional education, and in those rare instances when they do ask the advice of "outside experts," I suspect it is largely for symbolic purposes. Too often, educational leadership at the state level—official and unofficial—has been open to the charge that it was unwilling to examine public school needs critically.[22]

    [21] See also Roald I. Campbell and Donald H. Layton, *Policy Making for American Education* (Chicago: Midwest Administration Center, 1969), ch. 3. A full treatment of this process is Jay D. Scribner, "Impacts of Federal Programs on State Departments of Education," in Fuller and Pearson, vol. 2, ch. 11.
    [22] James B. Conant, *Shaping Educational Policy* (New York: McGraw-Hill, 1964), 37–38.

In fact, because there have been no comprehensive studies of the political role of the SDE's and CSSO's or of their impact on local educational agencies,[23] it is not possible to verify Conant's observation. But the evidence is more than suggestive that he was correct. We know that in the past many CSSO's derived the bulk of their political support from key local superintendents, and probably owed their appointments or nomination for election to them as well as to leading professors of educational administration. Bowles's evidence suggests that the CSSO emerges not as a top influential but as a unity candidate who supports rather than initiates policy.[24] As teacher and administrator groups have begun to compete, however, this monolithic structure has been breaking up. We simply do not know how CSSO's are chosen or nominated now. It appears that fewer governors and politicians are willing to listen to the advice of the professional education organizations, but their influence in selection of the CSSO is an open question.

Undoubtedly, the main movement for SDE's is toward more control and influence over local districts. For many years this state agency responded to its constituency of professional education interest groups and of malapportioned state legislatures, both favoring rural areas. The increasing role of state and federal aid, however, is bringing more attention to the cities and hence to an increased SDE role throughout the state.

The federal influence on the growth and reorientation of the SDE has been dramatic since 1965. Title V of the Elementary and Secondary Education Act of 1965 provided support for increasing the state professional staff, usually doubling it, as we see in Table 2. Three-fourths of the present staffs of all states have been in their jobs less than three years.[25] While Title V could be used flexibly for non-federal program services, other titles included a federal allocation for state administrative functions. The result in one large state department was that 16 of its 26 departments were devoting all or

[23] An exploratory analysis on this topic is David L. Colton, "State Power and Local Decision Making in Education," paper presented to the American Educational Research Association meeting, 1969, and indirectly the studies cited in [Joseph M. Schlesinger, "The Politics of the Executive," in Herbert Jacob and Kenneth Vines (eds.), *Politics in the American State* (Boston: Little, Brown, 1965)]. The SDE is headed in six states by an appointed official, in twenty-three by an independent board, and in twenty-one by an elected official; see *Book of the States, 1964–1965* (Chicago: Council of State Governments, 1965).

[24] B. Dean Bowles, "The Power Structure in State Education Politics," *Phi Delta Kappan*, 49 (1968), 337–40.

[25] See source in Table 2, at 15. The annual reports of this Advisory Council provide good longitudinal data on personnel changes in state education agencies.

TABLE 2   IMPACT ON STATE EDUCATIONAL STAFF SIZE FROM FEDERAL FUNDS, 1962 AND 1968

State	Professional Positions	
	1962	1968
Alabama	43	140
Minnesota	100	154
New Jersey	69	197
New York	277	557
Rhode Island	35	61
South Dakota	19	58
Texas	173	300
Utah	38	77
Vermont	29	73

Source: Advisory Council on State Departments of Education, *The State of State Departments of Education* (Washington, D.C.: Government Printing Office, 1969), 15–32.

part of their attention to federally related programs, and 64 of the 135 professional personnel were involved in federal projects.[26]

In short, the new national legislation has made SDE's even more dependent upon federal funds. These officials lament the expanding federal role in their affairs but in most cases cannot get money from the state legislature and governor to expand their staffs. One long-time observer of SDE summarized the current situation this way.

Most . . . , instead of interacting with federal agencies and even with local school districts as equals in a major enterprise, appear to be simply responding to forces about them. [SDE's] engage chiefly in regulatory activities as required by their respective state legislatures. Responses to the federal legislation have been of the same general nature; when functions are imposed by Title I and Title II of the ESEA and the Vocational Act, they are more or less willingly assumed. More and more the agendas of most [SDE's] are being set by the federal government.[27]

One counterthrust has been the formation of the Education Commission of the States to improve their coordinated action and studies.[28] The commission, presently representing forty-two states, ad-

[26] Campbell and Layton, 55.
[27] Ibid., 56.
[28] See Michael D. Usdan. "The Role and Future of State Educational Coalitions," *Educational Administration Quarterly*, 5 (1969), 26–42; and Allan M. Carter, "The Shaping of the Compact for Education," *Educational Record* (Washington, D.C.: American Council on Education, 1966).

ministers the National Assessment of Education program. The initial hope was that a group of states could exert more influence in federal relations by presenting united views on policy issues. But although the compact has become more of a forum for discussing common problems, it has failed to develop a mandate to lobby in Washington in order to transmit specific demands to federal leaders.

Reviewing the impact of these recent changes, it is appropriate to ask whether SDE's have now become merely extensions of the federal government. We note in response that the value orientation of representatives of different levels of the federal system are frequently not the same.[29] This is especially important because administration of federal grants by the states requires program judgments by state officers. For example, what types of vocational or compensatory programs should have preference? Which local districts are most in need of funds? By contrast, the bulk of the state-provided aid is distributed automatically through a legislative formula based on such factors as average daily attendance, assessed value per pupil, and local tax effort. The SDE's function is merely to compute the formula and send money to local districts, unlike its role in federal funds where it has more flexibility. Although new program discretions are given with federal funds, Table 2 suggests also the growth in SDE resources provided by Washington. This interaction is important enough, however, that in a later chapter [of the original book] we will focus on the politics of intergovernmental relations and consider in detail the implications for federalism of the issues discussed above.

STATE SUBSYSTEMS

The conversion systems that allocate educational resources at the state level do not operate independently of their environment. Much like their local counterparts, these political authorities are the object of demands for particular allocations of state resources that give priority to certain values. These demands are transferred from society to the political system by education interest groups and by citizen participation in elections and referenda. We turn, then, to considering how such demands are mobilized, aggregated, and articulated.

[29] For empirical evidence, see U.S. Senate Committee on Government Operations, Intergovernmental Relations Subcommittee, *The Federal System as Seen by State and Local Officials* (1963).

INTEREST GROUPS

Since board members have few strong views on specific policies and SDE's have traditionally responded to rather than exercised leadership, the impact of interest groups has been substantial. They have not only been the principal advocates for increased state aid, but have provided support for preserving what they deem to be professional considerations in such regulatory areas as curriculum and certification.

The most important single interest group has been the state teachers association—the National Education Association affiliate. Although it has grown rapidly in big cities, the American Federation of Teachers has not concentrated its lobbying or organizational efforts at the state level. As in other areas of state politics, the state NEA affiliates differ considerably in the amount of political pressure they can exert. The Texas State Teachers Association, for example, is strong enough to commit state legislators to its salary proposals during the campaigns or primary elections; it has been notably successful in overriding the Texas governor's budget recommendations. On the other hand, the California Teachers Association has been unable to commit a majority of the state legislature to its school finance proposals.

The importance of teacher groups for generating demands in the political system was substantiated by a study of three large-membership state affiliates in the Midwest.

The groups and individuals who articulate the policy proposals, the innovators, so to speak, are those who have a direct and tangible stake in the outcome of the decisions. . . . [I]n each of the states we surveyed the major group was the state affiliate of the National Education Association. . . . These groups have a relatively high degree of organization, a principal spokesman, a wealth of information about school needs, and generally favorable access to at least some points in the formal decision-making structure.[30]

All three of these groups presented information about school needs by stressing the "objectivity" and expertness of their educational analyses. They avoided identifying, allying, or competing with groups not directly concerned with education. In short, the image was of professionals "above politics," expert and objective. Anything beyond persuasion through testimony was regarded as

[30] Masters et al., 268–69.

"desperate" or "critical"; avoiding these labels hopefully separated the teachers from charges that their views were politically inspired. At such "critical" times, however, the capitol could be flooded with telegrams and letters from school professionals supporting the NEA views.[31]

This does not mean, however, that the demands of teachers associations are always, or in some states frequently, converted into policy outputs. In large part the result has depended on the cohesion and competition of the various education lobbies, as we shall shortly see. In some states, moreover, the NEA affiliate lacks aggressive leadership, is hobbled by poor relations with the governor's office (where the budget is formulated), and competes with a large, city-based AFT. Further, the power of teachers is not always credible. Some politicians suspect that much of the membership belongs to NEA only because belonging to it is a professional norm, and that the leadership cannot mobilize the teachers to vote against politicians who do not follow the teachers' advice.[32]

Teachers are not the only statewide education interest groups. There often exists an affiliate for school administrators that has divorced itself from the NEA teacher affiliate. For instance, the Michigan Association of School Administrators (MASA) represents 96 percent of the city superintendents and assistant superintendents. It retains a formal affiliation with NEA, but its viewpoint is usually somewhat different.[33] The administrators association's influence lies in the nature of its membership—school superintendents are highly respected members of their communities with an image as local experts on education. Consequently, they enjoy easier access to state legislators than do teachers. In Michigan, the NEA is regarded by the legislature more as a teacher-welfare bargaining agent. MASA officials use the tactic of making sure that the contact with legislatures is locally initiated, related only to the specific local tax situation, and is not a statewide lobbying effort. Again, the objective is to have the membership be seen as educators, not politicians. This orientation leads, however, to a lack of political sophistication and interest by the members, as substantiated by the executive secretary's

---

[31] For a categorization of influence patterns, see Laurence Iannaccone, *Politics in Education* (New York: Center for Applied Research in Education, 1967). For a good case study of such tactics, see Michael D. Usdan, *The Political Power of Education in New York State* (New York: Teachers College Press, Columbia University, 1963).

[32] See Alan Rosenthal, *Pedagogues and Power* (Syracuse: Syracuse University Press, 1969), ch. 1.

[33] Masters et al., 187–90.

belief that his biggest problem was "getting our boys interested." [34]

Another politically active organization in some states is the affiliate of the National School Boards Association. The national office is hindered in its political activities by the conflicting interests of 19,300 heterogeneous local school boards. Probably 90 percent of the local school board members in any state, however, belong to the state affiliate. As more of the governing authority has shifted to the state, board members have organized in order to gain access to the new points of decision. State school board associations, unlike their professional education counterparts, do not maintain large staffs or generate policy proposals. Rather, they act as watchdogs over public school legislation introduced by others and then provide support or opposition. School board associations view themselves as not being on the public payroll and consequently as acting in the best interests of education. Since school boards represent both the schools and the taxpayers, the associations contend they should represent schools at the state capitol instead of public school employees. In some states, such as Michigan, this orientation has led to rivalry between the two types of interest groups. For example, as teacher groups stress salary increases in state budgets, school board associations may hold out for a broader focus. [35]

Another potential lay interest group is the state affiliate of the National Congress of Parents and Teachers. The PTA's size alone is a source of some strength because it includes hundreds of thousands of voters in large states. However, not having a natural degree of cohesion, it is a reluctant entrant, especially in partisan situations. The mass of PTA members are rarely stimulated to such militant action as letter writing and phone calls, but the association does use face-to-face contact between its leadership and the state legislators. In short, politicians find the PTA a useful friend but not a bothersome enemy.

None of the studies have found an organized, statewide, interest group with the primary objective of *opposing* increases in state aid for the schools. Bailey and his associates found in New England that the opposition consisted of business groups, representatives of rural localism, and conservative politicians and citizens concerned

---

[34] Ibid., 189.

[35] For a perspective on this rivalry from the standpoint of big cities, see Alan K. Campbell, "Socio-Economic, Political, and Fiscal Environment of Educational Policy Making in Large Cities," in Michael W. Kirst (ed.), *The Politics of Education* (Berkeley: McCutchan, 1970), 300–17. For contrast, see Tom Wiley, *Politics and Purse Strings in New Mexico's Public Schools* (Albuquerque: University of New Mexico Press, 1968).

about any policy to increase state taxes substantially. State aid to education is usually such a large percentage of total state expenditures that any significant increase in education assistance will arouse opposition from some groups. But standing or *ad hoc* organizations do not function primarily for the purpose of holding down school costs to the state. To be against public education is not considered a viable or desirable political strategy. Rather, opposition is expressed in terms of the high, overall, state tax burden or the threat to local autonomy. Increasingly, we hear complaints that no one knows the output likely to result from increases in state aid to education. An increase in teachers' salaries through more state aid does not necessarily cause higher student achievement or better pupil attitudes. The opponents' arguments are expressed in terms of a skepticism that more money will result in their definition of "better education. . . ."

chapter five

Local school governance

MARIO FANTINI, MARILYN GITTELL, AND
RICHARD MAGAT

ANATOMY OF SCHOOL BOARDS

. . . The commonplace target of attempts to reform or re-
juvenate the school has been the school board, which is the legally
designated decision-making body and the agent of the highest education authority in the state, the regents or the state board of
education or public instruction, as the bodies are known.

Assuming, for a moment, that school boards are, in fact, the
governors of the schools, what are their characteristics? One attri-
bute common to boards is that they are unpaid lay members of the
community. No major school system is presently governed by paid
professionals equivalent to the city manager or by paid commis-
sioners.[1] Some school boards are elected, others appointed. Most
large cities—New York, until now, having been the largest exception—elect their boards. However, the elections are at large, a
factor, as will be noted later, that is crucial to the crisis of accountability in urban education. In more quiescent times, especially in
smaller communities, a tradition of nonpartisanship was followed
in school board elections, generally held in election off-years. The
schools were said to be above politics, and, often, small, self-
appointed groups of civic leaders chose one of their own number
to stand for election, the prestige of the group being strong enough
so that their choice was, generally, unopposed. Such benign selec-

"Local School Governance" (editors' title). From Mario Fantini, Marilyn Git-
tell, and Richard Magat, *Community Control and the Urban School* (New York:
Praeger Publishers, Inc., 1970), pp. 62–76. Reprinted by permission of Praeger
Publishers, Inc., and the authors.

[1] Under 1969 legislation, however, New York City board members are paid on
a *per diem* basis.

tion is now largely a thing of the past, except in the most homogeneous and affluent suburbs.

Another reflection of the unique status of the school board as an arm of government is, in nonelective systems, appointment by a political authority—by a mayor, say, or, as in Philadelphia until 1966, by a group of judges. Appointment still is the method of school board selection in one-fourth of the large- and medium-sized city school districts. It is an approach that, presumably, insulates the school board from the partisanship associated with election contests but, in practice, it often places the matter squarely into the political realm. To mediate direct political influence, reformers seem to favor another system—the interposition of a screening mechanism into the appointment process. This system, presumably, obliges the mayor or other appointing authority to choose school board members from a pool of candidates screened and certified as capable and willing. The panel itself may be composed of prestigious and influential members of the community—college presidents and heads of civic organizations, for example. The final choice in this two-stage process, then, is political only in the sense that it is made by the mayor. It is presumed to be basically nonpartisan because the mayor is permitted to choose only candidates certified by civic leaders as having the best interests of the community at heart. The shift from direct mayoral appointment to appointment through a screening panel was viewed as a significant reform in urban school processes. Chicago and Philadelphia have adopted the panel process, and New York City similarly changed its system, as a result of an act of the 1961 state legislature that, following a series of school-construction scandals, removed the incumbent board. New legislation in 1969 switched New York to a mainly elective system (for five of seven members). A study by one of the authors indicated that, in practice, the selection panel made little difference in the appointments in any of the cities that used it.

Until recently, the focus of discussion of school-board selection and composition was on procedural matters. The pros and cons of elective vs. appointive methods were extensively debated. Those favoring elected boards argued for the ultimate fairness and wisdom of voting as a democratic process; taking the bad elective choices with the good was as much worth the risk in school government as in the government of the state or nation, they maintained. Proponents of appointed boards, on the other hand, said analogies with elected political office were unwarranted. Membership on a school board pays nothing, for one thing. For another, education is a unique function, in which the contention and partisanship that accompany elections ought to be avoided. Furthermore, high-minded men and women might be discouraged from serving on school boards if they had to go through the trouble, expense, and possible personal abuse of an election. Rarely argued, however, were the questions of how substantial the authority of the school board actually was and how representative a central school board —elected or appointed *at large*—could be, especially in large and ethnically and racially diverse areas.

If a community is an organic whole, with a single public interest in education, there is little reason to serve subcommunity, "selfish" interests by guaranteeing particular groups in the community (labor, ethnic minorities, etc.) seats on the board of education. But, in cities where the nonwhite proportion of the general population has grown and where the nonwhite proportion of the public school population has increased even more sharply, nonwhites are under-represented on citywide school boards. The proportionate volume of nonwhite voting is still substantially below that of other groups. Moreover, white communities are generally better organized to elect their candidates, particularly in citywide elections. Minorities also tend to be underrepresented in appointive boards. In either case, the result, commonly, is a lack of accountability, of responsiveness to the needs of the nonwhite community—or, almost as important, a lack of *belief* within the nonwhite community that a body on which it is not represented, or is poorly represented, can be responsive.

For that reason, then, Negroes in some cities have proposed that the boards be elected on a district basis, to more accurately reflect the needs of the people in the community. A school board member elected at large, they argue, by virtue of being responsible to everybody, is really responsible to nobody, and where there is no responsibility, there is no responsiveness.

Regardless of the method of election, the composition of school boards in urban areas is markedly different from the over-all population of most large cities, and the contrast is even starker if the board is compared in its makeup to the parents of the children in the public schools.

Throughout the country, school board members, whether appointed or elected, have more formal education by far than the average for all citizens. For the most part, the members of the boards of education are recruited from the middle and upper classes, having established some prior role in political or educational circles. The last comprehensive national review of research, by the U.S. Office of Education in 1962, found that the larger the community, the higher the educational level of school board members. In districts of 25,000 pupils or more, for example, 72.6 per cent of the school board members had graduated from college, compared to 43.1 per cent of members in school districts with under 3,000 pupils (still above the 7.9 per cent of the total adult population who were college graduates). The average for all school boards was 48.3 per cent. Regional differences come into play, too: boards in the Northeast have the highest level of educational preparation, the South the lowest (though, again, higher than the national average for the total population). Only in the South, and there only by one measure, was any evidence found that elective boards contained significantly fewer less educated members than appointed bodies: 50.3 per cent of elected Southern boards had at least one member who did not graduate from high school, compared to only 27.7 per cent of appointed boards. At the other end of the scale, at least one college graduate was found on 88.6 per cent of the appointed boards, compared to 71.6 on the elected boards.

Business and professional people dominate school boards the country over, according to the Office of Education survey. They account for more than three-fifths of the members. Housewives account for 7.2 per cent and skilled and unskilled workers for 9.4 per cent. The highest proportion of business and professional membership (75.2 per cent) was found in larger school systems. In general, appointed boards had an even larger proportion of business and professional men and women than the elected ones.

In 1967, one of the authors examined school board composition in six major cities (Detroit, Chicago, Philadelphia, New York, Baltimore, and St. Louis). She found that two-thirds of the members of all the boards were over fifty years of age. Each board takes into account the need to represent ethnic and religious groups, but the typical Negro board member is, usually, a professional not intimately identified with civil rights causes. Detroit had the highest proportion of nonwhite members (two out of seven) and Chicago the lowest (two out of nine).

In all six, women board members are representatives of established women's civic groups. Each board includes representation of the three religious groups, although not necessarily in strict proportion to the population of the city. The religious balance appeared to be a more sensitive issue in New York City than in any of the other cities. The adoption of the panel-selection device in Philadelphia, New York, and Chicago had made little difference in the composition of the board as compared to earlier boards in the same cities or as compared to the boards of other cities.

Nearly three-fourths of all board members were college educated, and about half had advanced or professional degrees. The most common advanced degree of board members was the law degree. In each of the cities, at least one and usually more of the board members were lawyers. Chicago, New York, and Detroit had labor represented on the board, indicating the importance of unions in those cities. In St. Louis, labor was unrepresented on the board.

Detroit, Philadelphia, and St. Louis had religious leaders on the board. The business community was represented on five of the six boards, most heavily in St. Louis. New York City had six board members with a background in professional education, St. Louis and Baltimore had three members with an education background and Philadelphia had one. Teachers were not represented on any of the boards.

In another day, wide social and economic disparities between governing bodies and the electorate were not so suspect. But such benevolence does not prevail in a climate of educational failure and suspicion by low-income, minority communities of the effectiveness, and even the motives, of school authorities, especially when a large school system's power is concentrated at the center.

BUT WHO IS IN CHARGE?

As a result of recent research into school policy-making, a more subtle issue has now come to the fore: Is the school board in the large cities the strong branch of government its legislating and policy-making powers would appear to make it? Effective school board power is offset not only by such forces as accrediting agencies, the colleges and universities, and the National Education Association and its galaxy of professional education associations but also by centers of power closer to home. Other powerful agents in the government of schools are the teachers and administrators. The more complex and sprawling a school system, the more independent of the board a school bureaucracy may, in fact, be. The board, which seldom has much of a staff directly and wholly responsible to itself, must rely on the superintendent and other school professionals for most of its information and recommendations. Weakness or ineffectuality of a board of education is, in part attributed to this lack of staff and to the limited time available to board members as part-time, unsalaried officials. Joseph Pois, a

Chicago school board member, in his book *The School Board Crisis,* notes the frustrations of school board members in the face of overwhelming problems and the lack of time and resources. Often, the school board will be caught up in a minor administrative problem and neglect long-range policy issues.

But, even in their own domain, policy-making, school boards often are not the final masters. As a visible and handy target, the superintendent himself is not likely to subvert or delay implementation of board policies, for, if his opposition is too blatant, the board has the ready remedy of its power of removal. Undercutting by the rest of the professional bureaucracy, however, is another matter. By inertia alone or non–decision-making, they can thwart board intentions. In several studies of school integration in New York City, the failure of the bureaucracy to implement board policy has been shown as decisive in the final outcome.

With respect to parents and civic groups concerned with city-wide educational policies, the administrators, having both control of information and insulation from public accountability, can effectively fence off the public from an influential voice in policies and practices in a variety of functions, from budget-making to curriculum.

Various organizations of principals, district superintendents, and other administrators in the New York system banded together in 1963 in a Council of Supervisory Associations, which, from time to time, has engaged in open rebellion—including lobbying, newspaper advertising, and other techniques of persuasion—against policies of their own chief administrator (the superintendent of schools) and the board of education. Supervisory and administrative dominance of decision-making in other cities, in some degree or other, has been attested to in several studies.

Large-city school systems are composed not only of vertical hierarchies of supervisors—from the superintendent of schools, at the pinnacle, to assistant principals or secondary-school department heads, at the bottom—but also of a horizontal structure of specialists. Specialists preside over dozens of services (such as audiovisual instruction), over curriculum areas (languages, the sciences, physical education, etc.) and, more recently, over involvement in federal aid programs. American schools are more lavishly administered than any in the world. James Koerner has remarked, "No other system can come even close to matching the numbers of full-time, non-teaching school administrators that run our local school systems . . . many of whom are more highly paid than state governors, university presidents, or our most distinguished scholars."

The specialists make policies for the system as a whole, implemented through headquarters-based directors to principals and field staff. In some cities, curriculum coordinators form a bridge between headquarters and the scene of action, but, often, the system flows—or crawls—in a stream of paper, some of it inhibiting, some of it ignored, and some of it irrelevant to many schools in the system.

Of course, any system with hundreds of employees, to say nothing of thousands, is, by definition, a bureaucracy. This term, of course need not be pejorative. But, as applied to school systems, it invariably has negative connotations. It is not the sheer size, alone, that casts the term in opprobrium. It is, also, the style of the specialists and the crisscrossing of levels of authority. In most large school systems, promotion to supervisory rank is defined not so much by genuine merit as by the trappings of merit—formalized credentials and prescribed standards. Too often, the credentials and standards, presumably designed to assure quality, have hardened into barriers and restraints, limiting promotion to men and women ready to conform to a rule-ridden system and tenacious enough to pass through fixed hurdles that are legitimized more by age than by purposes that meet the fundamental needs of the system's clients, the children. The more complex the rules of the game, the more it pays the players who aspire to success to have been on the scene from the beginning of their careers. Thus, the system does not need to erect formal fences against outsiders, although it often does. It is *de facto* exclusive and inbred. The structure is further complicated by a web of guildlike organizations of specialists—of department chairmen, of principals at the elementary and secondary levels, of guidance personnel, of secretaries. More often than not, the guilds' roots lie in school politics rather than in professional concerns. They function as lobbies to protect or advance their status as against that of other guilds. In many ways, these associations serve as participants in policy-making through public statements and direct pressure on the board of education and on city and state officials. "The school administration, not the local board and not the teachers, remains the primary focus of control over educational policy and over its implementation," Koerner says.

Thus does the professional educator wield his power. In benign circumstances, the gains of the entrenched professional bureaucracy do not inflict great losses on others—except, of course, to the taxpayer, who must meet the cost without guarantees against nonproductivity. But that is, after all, true in many civil service structures, and in private organizations, too. But, when the circumstances are dynamic—when, for example, the makeup of the student population has changed drastically, or the society is gripped by social upheavals—the system then exacts a far greater toll. For changing clients and changing circumstances call for changes in the system, and a highly structured, inbred, and protective system does not change voluntarily. Usually, when change is thrust upon it, it accommodates only after bitter resistance. In such a contest, the other parties—in the case of schools, children and their parents —are lacking in power, initially unorganized, and easily intimidated by the authority of the professional. That is the political setting of the movement for community control, although, as noted elsewhere, the educational underpinnings are quite as powerful, if not ultimately overriding.

ADMINISTRATIVE DECENTRALIZATION

Over the years, the administrative staffs of urban school systems have increased in complexity and in numbers, the latter increase disproportionate to that of the student population. To alleviate the sheer weight of sprawling headquarters staff, many large-city school systems have established field administrative units, which may range in number from three (Baltimore) to thirty (New York). Mounting concern in recent years with an allegedy unresponsive headquarters staffs has resulted in the delegation of somewhat increased discretion in decision-making to field administrators. In other words, some administrative decentralization has been under way.

However, the mere delegation of responsibility is not a guarantor of responsiveness to community needs and desires. There is no redistribution of power under these arrangements. First, head-quarters personnel retain strong controls over citywide policy. These administrators, in general, are the products of strict merit and seniority systems. Even a reform-oriented superintendent of schools often cannot choose his own administrative assistants and personnel staff. He must rely on people who have risen within the system.

Analysts of a reform administration in the Philadelphia public schools, for example, noted that the new superintendent, Mark Shedd, while he brought in a group of young, bright assistants, picked the top bureaucrats as his own men:

He left the old Establishment intact. And the Establishment was not going to move the system forward. Some say that Shedd did not so much select these people as just close his eyes to their existence. There is a considerable body of thought in Philadelphia that the only way to truly deal with the administration building is to bury it. It contains 1,500 people, many of whom could be stacked in drawers and never missed.

In most urban school districts, the administrative hierarchy comes from the teaching ranks. Promotion to headquarters is based on either further required examination or experience as a school administrator. This procedure closes off the system to outsiders and nonschool administrators. Headquarters staff are generally experienced field personnel who have been promoted into these positions. With very few exceptions, nobody can be a superintendent of schools in the United States—no matter how distinguished he may be intellectually or as an administrator of other public institutions —who has not been through a stipulated training program in a school of education.

Further, there are limitations on the policy-making delegated locally to field administrators. And, even given some delegated authority, district officers still have an eye cocked upward, to headquarters and administrative superiors, and not across, to the community they are assigned to serve. Their eyes tend toward the distant, high direction even when decentralization includes local advisory boards of education. For example, years before murmurs of community control began in New York City, the board of education established a system of appointed local school boards. Although these boards have, at times, provided a useful forum for discussing school-site selection and other subjects, and, sometimes, exerted decisive influence on substantive matters, they have lacked decision-making power. They could hold no one *responsible*—not the district administrator, not the central authority—for the performance of the schools in their district.

Martin Mayer, who served on a district school board in New York City for five years, has described the dead end to which many dedicated men and women have come under this structure: ". . . there was almost nothing I could do for the people who called me, and little of substance could come out of our meeting. . . . This giant empire is almost completely insulated from public control." Leading civic organizations, notably the Public Education Association, the Women's City Club, and the United Parents Association, have commented on the lack of community participation available under the advisory boards. And, as recently as 1968, a report of the board of education's own advisory committee on decentralization said that, despite the latest improvements in *administrative* decentralization, a sampling of local advisory boards showed the vast majority of members did not feel their advice was significantly influencing the district superintendent's actions. The conclusion was based on a nine-month survey of five districts varying in socio-economic composition but each having some contact with "disadvantaged" children.

Many local school boards, the report noted, were experiencing difficulty in overcoming professional inability or unwillingness to relate to the parental and subcommunity groups. Although district administrators were quoted as approving the concept of administrative decentralization, they expressed fears even over the increased status of the existing local school boards, which were a far cry from what proponents of full decentralization and meaningful community participation have in mind.

Most professionals (not just those in education) would prefer to be left alone by laymen. The public ideology of school professionals is that parents are apathetic about education, that, if they cared more and took a more lively interest in their schools, their children would do better. Such attitudes apply particularly to ghetto parents, whose poor attendance records at PTA meetings is often the object of tongue-clucking by school personnel and by "interested" middle-class parents.

The parent associations sometimes contribute to incidental improvements and occasionally exert pressure or persuasion on a substantive curricular matter. But their power is quite limited. Fundamentally, they are another reinforcement of the system and its needs, as distinct from the needs of students, which do not always coincide. PTA's are ridiculed for cake sales and preoccupation with trivia and sociability, but their effect is far more significant, in the negative sense. They exist as an elaborate structure at the local, district, state, and national levels, enrolling millions of members and putting forward the illusion of parent representation in public education. The effect of all this is regressive in at least two ways. First, it has often preempted or precluded the formation of other public groups with a direct policy role. Second, it has been supportive of the prevailing educational order.

Teacher organizations and unions have proliferated over the last several years and have emerged as another significant professional influence in school affairs. Although financially weaker than the NEA (a $2 million annual budget in 1967 compared to an estimated NEA budget of $25 million), the American Federation of Teachers is growing in strength; it has more than 650 chapters, and, beginning in the late 1960's, conducted strikes in several large and medium-sized cities. Union leaders have become important participants in school policy-making, and the union contract is one of the more important documents of school policy, particularly in such matters as working conditions, salaries, and fringe benefits. Priorities for the allocation of school funds are greatly influenced by the settlement of wage and salary levels for teachers. In several of the larger cities, unions and other teacher organizations have been directly involved in other related areas of school policy, often with the result that such provisions become an integral part of the contract arrangement. Such matters as team teaching, class size, and compensatory educational programs are becoming issues for negotiation. The American Federation of Teachers, in fact, has adopted a national policy favoring the More Effective Schools program (the compensatory education program initiated by the United Federation of Teachers in New York) and is seeking its adoption in several cities. Teacher organizations and unions have worked with school administrators on problems of recruitment and training as well.

The confrontation between the union and the ghetto community in New York City over the community-control issue indicated the enormous power that the union could exercise on local and state officials when it felt compelled to do so. There is no question but that teachers' unions have emerged as major participants in the politics of education in urban areas.

In addition to the formal organizations of professionals in urban communities, some important informal participants group together to influence school policy-making. Special education interest groups are usually reform-oriented citizens who watch over the school system on a citywide basis. Some have a small professional staff to carry on organizational or public relations activities, and they occasionally engage their own researchers for particular studies, some of which have proved valuable. More often, though, these groups support the system and serve to help in securing more funds for school purposes. They are seldom critical of the total system but may attack a particular program or encourage adoption of a new approach or project. Boards of education, superintendents and school administrators are usually in close contact with these groups and use their good offices to reinforce their own positions. On occasion, there is an interchange of personnel as well. In New York, for example, the former chief executives of two main education interest groups are now employed by the board of education.

Since racial integration became a lively issue in public education, civil rights and *ad hoc* local groups in urban areas have, also, become directly involved in education issues. In fact, many of the school systems have established human relations divisions to cope with the increasing pressures in this area. While civil rights groups have concerned themselves largely with the integration issue, they are, also, more directly involved than other citizen groups with other matters related to minority groups and compensatory educational needs. Their influence has, however, been of limited effect.

The analysis of power in school policy-making is particularly relevant to the movement for school reform—primarily because the concentration of power in the central bureaucracy in urban school systems is so basic to the lack of responsiveness of the system to changing circumstances and needs, but also because it greatly influences the ability to achieve change. Those in power have a vested interest in maintaining the system, while those who are powerless are striving to effect adjustments to allow their voices to be heard.

Community frustration with the public education system has manifested itself in the movement toward the community school, and this movement, of course, fits in with a general effort to achieve a redistribution of power to allow the public a greater voice in the development of educational policy.

c h a p t e r   s i x

Social class analysis and the control of public education

W. W. CHARTERS, JR.

I. INTRODUCTION

"American public school systems support the values of the 'dominant' social class of their constituent communities."

This is the proposition currently emerging from half a century of research on the social control of American public education. As early as 1927, George Counts observed that the control of schools rests in the hands of persons "drawn from the more favored economic and social classes," a fact which "inevitably" shapes the nature of the educative process in the school (6). The proliferation of research studies since 1927 has expanded the empirical support for the proposition. In his recent summary of stratification in education, Stephenson refers to the now-documented fact that teachers, as well as board members, "are recruited from the middle segments of our stratification system," and he is able to point to accumulated evidence indicating that the general culture of the school "tends to be representative of the middle and upper stratification positions rather than the lower" (10). Brown extends the proposition with his assertion that the education system "in any country and at all periods reflects the values of the ruling class" (2, p. 249). The proposition is phrased differently by different writers, but the basic ingredient is the same: schools serve the interests of certain select

From W. W. Charters, Jr., "Social Class Analysis and the Control of Public Education," *Harvard Educational Review,* 23 (Fall, 1953), pp. 268–79, 283. Copyright © 1953 by President and Fellows of Harvard College. Reprinted by permission of the *Harvard Educational Review* and the author.

Numbers in parentheses refer to the bibliography at the end of the article.

groups in the community, groups which we have referred to here as the "dominant class." [1]

For many educators, the proposition virtually has achieved the status of a scientifically demonstrated principle. Its proponents are respectable scholars, writing directly in the current of a major intellectual movement in social science. Their argument is documented with impressive data obviously resulting from hard, devoted field investigation. Moreover, the argument frequently is cast in readable, persuasive prose.

There is no wonder that the proposition has excited discussion and concern among professional educators. It holds serious implications for the role of the school in American society. Persons who believe the school should play a creative part in our society are confronted with research findings which seem to say that it cannot. How is it possible, they ask, to apply a classless science of pedagogy in the nation's classrooms when teachers are dominated by their middle-class origins? Can administrators ever function in a leadership capacity or must they always serve faithfully their dominant class masters? If the proposition is a scientific principle, with the universal application which is characteristic of scientific principles, the education profession must relinquish its visions of the school as a positive force in society.

In view of the serious implications of the proposition, it is important to examine carefully the kind of evidence which supports its claim to scientific validity. It is likewise important to ask whether or not the social class analysis on which the proposition is based is adequate to provide the kinds of principles concerning the school's relation to the community which we might legitimately expect from a scientific analysis. This article cannot undertake such a comprehensive task. We shall restrict ourselves to a consideration of social stratification as it bears on the administrative and policy forming aspects of the school. If the proposition is true that schools reflect the values of the dominant class, the process by which this occurs should be observable in the operations by which the school charts

[1] A striking variation is found among writers in the specification of the particular groups whose interests the school serves. Each of the following have been mentioned as constituting the select group (or, as we say, the "dominant class"): (a) the ruling class, (b) large property holders, (c) agents of major financial and economic interests, (d) business and professional men, (e) the middle, the upper-middle, or the upper class. The criterion of stratification implied in these varies remarkably. The first usage is based on a criterion of political power, the second and third on a criterion of economic power, the fourth on some criterion of occupational rank, and the last on a criterion of prestige ranking insofar as the class is identified according to the system proposed by Lloyd Warner.

and pursues its course. Indeed, a substantial part of the support for the proposition is drawn from research purporting to show that a dominant class bias exists in the school's decision-making and administrative organs. Hence, we are able to examine the major part of the evidence commonly cited as demonstration of the proposition even from our restricted vantage point.[2]

II. EVIDENCE FOR THE DOMINANT CLASS CONTROL OF THE SCHOOL

Two distinct lines of empirical research lend evidence to support the argument that public school systems of America are controlled by the dominant class of their respective communities. One line— in the academic field of educational research—is identified with the name of George Counts; the other line is identified with the sociological community studies of Lloyd Warner. Where the studies of Counts and his progeny are extensive in the number of school systems investigated, those of Warner and his associates are intensive in the few systems they encountered in the course of their community analyses. Among the sociological community studies, investigations of the control of school systems are only a by-product of a more immediate interest in the class bias of the educational service provided children in the community, which in turn is only a part of a treatise on the entire community stratification pattern. Nevertheless, data contributed by the two lines of research serve identical functions in the argument that schools are controlled by the dominant class.

THE SOCIAL COMPOSITION OF SCHOOL BOARDS

If it can be shown that the persons who control school systems— particularly school board officials—are members of the community's dominant class, then it is possible to conclude that the school is shaped in the image of the dominant class. This reasoning was made clear by Counts when he wrote that "the nature of the school must inevitably reflect the forces that control it" and proceeded to investigate the class positions occupied by members of boards of education across the country (6).

---

[2] Types of evidence which we shall not cover relate to such matters as the class bias of rewards and punishments in classroom, class differentials in pupil adjustment to and success in the school culture, class selectivity of school dropouts, and class orientations of curricula.

Counts determined the class position of board members through the occupations they pursued in civil life. He found that over three-quarters of the several thousand members of city school boards for whom he had information were business or professional men, persons whom he regarded as representatives of the dominant class.[3] By virtue of their "favored" positions in society, Counts asserted, such individuals are conservative and defensive in the face of change; this fact necessarily reflects upon the prevailing characteristics of the school systems.

If there were any doubt about Counts' findings concerning the occupations of board members, they have been completely dispelled by now. The author has located 62 separate studies which have investigated board member occupations in a wide variety of school districts, including two replications of Counts' nation-wide research, and none depart in any important way from the results which Counts exhibits.[4] While the proportions of farmers-professionals-businessmen vary from study to study, these three groups universally constitute a substantial majority of board personnel.

Some investigators have attempted to determine the class position of board members through information concerning their economic conditions—their income, real estate holdings, and so forth —but such data are inconclusive, as a rule, since the researchers fail to compare them with the economic conditions of the community residents.

The recent sociological community studies tend to go into greater detail concerning the social positions of school board members, describing their occupational and social ties, their personal attributes, and their social class memberships.[5] Using the Warner system of social placement, these studies find board members typically to be in the upper-middle class. Of 18 board members in three communities (Old City, Hometown, and Yankee City), 13 are placed in the upper-middle class and four in the upper classes; the remaining

[3] Members of county, state, and college boards of education were even more preponderantly business or professional men. His data on rural school districts indicated that 95 per cent of the members were engaged in agriculture. The system of occupational classification he used did not allow him to distinguish farmers of the dominant class from other farmers; consequently, his data concerning rural boards do not contribute to his argument.

[4] A bibliography of these and other school board studies will be supplied by the author on request. A brief description of 16 such studies can be found in M. D. Crouse, "The Social Status of School Board Members in Huron County, Michigan," Unpublished Master's Thesis, University of Michigan, 1936.

[5] See, for example, the detail into which Hollingshead goes concerning the seven members of Elmtown's school board. (8, p. 124).

board member is identified as a member of the lower-middle class (12, Table XII, p. 118). The informal descriptions of board members usually include comments concerning their economic and political power positions in the community, although these are not systematically pursued.

The conclusion is hard to escape that board members are recruited from among business and professional men (except in rural areas) or, in different language, from among persons in the upper-middle class of the community.

Does this conclusion mean, as Counts assumed, that schools are under the direction of persons who reflect the conservative attitudes associated with "favored" class membership? Despite the popularity of attitude research in many educational fields, there is a distinct lack of research bearing on this question. Arnett found, in one of the few relevant studies, a relatively high level of conservatism among board members across the nation (1, chs. 9–10). But certain of his detailed findings are antithetical to Counts' assumption. He reports that professional men are more progressive in their attitudes toward social issues than any other occupational group represented on school boards; clerical workers are least progressive. Members with high incomes are more progressive on the whole than members with low incomes. Certain methodological inadequacies, however, prevent us from placing full confidence in Arnett's conclusions, and more studies are necessary to evaluate the propriety of Counts' assumption.[6] Arnett's findings, taken at face value, give rise to two interpretations: either the wealthy and professional men on boards failed to reflect the conservative dominant class values or they truly reflected the dominant class values but these values were not conservative.

For the sake of argument, let us suppose that board members do hold attitudes which reflect the values of the dominant class of

---

[6] Tests of conservatism are difficult to construct. There is sufficient research now to state positively that conservatism cannot be described on a single dimension; a man who is conservative on one type of social issue may be progressive on other types of issues. Moreover, the definition of a conservative stand on social issues is notoriously dependent upon political and intellectual trends of the time. Arnett used Harper's test of social beliefs which includes such a diversity of items, covering attitudes toward American policy in Latin America, toward the development of hydroelectric power, toward the importance of psychology in teacher education, and so on, that an aggregate score of "conservatism" or "non-conservatism" loses meaning. Much of Arnett's analysis consists of item by item comparison of responses of board members, classified by sex, age, occupation, income, etc., but his failure to include statistical tests of significance makes it impossible to separate differences due to chance error from truly meaningful differences.

the community, whether conservative or otherwise. What evidence is there that the attitudes they hold as *community citizens* enter into the decisions they reach as *officers of the school board?* In a noteworthy doctoral thesis, Campbell examined the votes cast by board officers in twelve Western cities and found no clear relationship between the stands taken by the officers of school legislation of social import and their social class positions in the community (as measured by their occupation and income) (3). It is entirely possible that a man who becomes a school board official will speak and vote (and even think) differently from the way he did as a community citizen. The social role of a responsible public officer imposes upon a man obligations and informal forces far different from those imposed upon him in the role of a relatively anonymous community citizen. The crucial question we must ask of Counts is whether or not the values of the dominant class enter into the decision-making process which board members engage in and which shapes the nature of the educational program in our public schools.

THE SOCIAL STATUS OF ADMINISTRATORS

How do school administrators contribute to the dominant class control of education? Far less empirical research or theoretical exposition exists on the contribution of administrators than on the contribution of board members to dominant class control.

The few attempts to explore the question (found in the sociological community studies) usually follow the same reasoning applied to school board investigations: if it can be shown that administrators are members of the community's dominant class, then schools can be expected to reflect the dominant class values. On this theme, the Gardners noted that the superintendent of schools in Old City occupied a position in the upper-middle class of the community (7). The most extensive commentary on the social position of administrators is in the case studies of two Yankee City educators—the superintendent and a principal (12, ch. 10). Both are described as upper-middle class members, although the superintendent is moving into the lower-upper class. The case studies purport to show that the manner in which the administrator performs his official duties is determined by the attitudes and values he has internalized as a consequence either (a) of his current social class position in the community or (b) of the social class position he occupied in his childhood and youth. To demonstrate the interrelationship among attitudes, class position, and behavior, the authors cite episodes which indicate class bias in the administrator's behavior; in apposition to these episodes they set passages which describe the administrator's orientation to and participation in the social class structure of the community. Although this type of demonstration reads well and perhaps convincingly, it allows the investigator to select his evidence to prove his point.

A different type of analysis is found in some other community studies: instead of viewing the administrator as a member of the dominant class and thereby willingly cooperating with the board to maintain dominant class values in the school, the sociologists view the administrator as a passive agent who has no choice but to respond to the board and other representatives of the dominant class.

The superintendent comes into a pre-existing socio-cultural complex with all its local values, beliefs, prejudices, and ground rules of what "to do" and "not to do." He must adjust to, and become a part of, a social system he did not help create. He is compelled by the pressures around him to organize his thoughts and activities in accordance with the demands made upon him by the people who wield the power in the community (11, pp. 198–199).

According to this trend of reasoning, the administrator is an automaton who, because the school board has the power to dismiss and otherwise penalize him, mirrors the dominant class attitudes of the board members.

Hollingshead modifies this analysis slightly when he suggests that the administrator responds not only to the board and their fellow representatives of the dominant class but also to pressures from within the school and to his own professional standards with which he must live (8, p. 140 f.). He is not a passive mirror of the board but a human being with values of his own struggling to resolve the conflict in which he is placed by the myriad of cross-pressures operating on him. Although Hollingshead's modification of the analysis appears to be slight, it is highly significant in the argument that the dominant class controls the schools. The administrator's official behavior is the result of the manner in which he responds to the forces impinging upon him—some of which are in conflict with the forces emanating from the dominant class. To maintain the argument that the dominant class controls the school, the social class analysts must prove that the administrator's conflict is generally resolved in favor of the dominant class interests.

Whatever the type of analysis may be, the accumulation of empirical findings concerning the contribution of administrators to dominant class control of the school is not, at the present time, impressive. At the best, any one community study can provide evidence on three or four school administrators, and only a handful of community studies currently exist.[7]

THE MIDDLE-CLASS TEACHER

It is beyond the scope of this enquiry to examine in detail the manner in which teaching personnel contribute to the dominant class control of school policy. Nevertheless, in the end school policy is established by its operating personnel and it is not out of place to note that the social class analysts rely on the fact that teachers are predominantly of the middle class to fortify their argument concerning dominant class control.[8] (Writers rarely attach significance to the difference between the middle-class orientations of teachers and the upper-middle class orientations of board members.) The argument is the same for teachers as for board members: since teachers typically occupy positions in the middle class of the community (read, dominant class), then dominant class standards and mores prevail in the classroom as teachers perform their educative functions.

III. ADEQUACY OF SOCIAL CLASS ANALYSIS

In the foregoing section we briefly reviewed certain of the empirical investigations which have led contemporary writers to conclude that public schools in America reflect the values of the dominant class. A heavy burden of proof for this proposition lies in the ob-

[7] That the administrator's social status in the community does reflect upon his school behavior is suggested by the pilot study conducted by Melvin Seeman, "Some Status Correlates of Leadership," *Leadership in American Education*, Vol. XIII (Chicago: University of Chicago Press, 1950), Chapter V, pp. 40–50. The factor which is related to the administrator's behavior is not his social class membership but the differential between his economic and his social status. Seeman's findings support the hypothesis that "leaders who are described as being relatively high in social position while being relatively low in economic position will also be described as engaging in those leader behaviors which are resistive to change, since conservative status-quoism would be one way of protecting a relatively high social position which is not buttressed by a correspondingly high economic position."

[8] Allison Davis' statement that "95 out of every 100 teachers are from the middle socio-economic groups" is our authority for referring to the middle-class position of teachers as a fact. Cited in Theodore I. Lenn, "Social Class: Conceptual and Operational Significance for Education," *Journal of Educational Sociology*, Vol. 26, No. 2 (October, 1952), p. 57.

servation that board members, administrators, and classroom teachers can be classified as members of the community's dominant class. If the persons who are in immediate control of school policies entertain a bias in favor of the dominant class, the educative process must reflect the bias. In comparison with many accepted propositions in educational sociology, the amount of research relating to this proposition is considerable. It is necessary now to examine the assumptions underlying the argument which is advanced to support the proposition.

ASSUMPTIONS IN THE ARGUMENT

Let us begin our examination of the series of interlocking assumptions implicit in the argument with the recognition that a school officer occupies a position in two distinct social structures—that of the community and that of the school institution within the community. The argument asserts that forces impinging upon a person by virtue of his position in the community social structure determine the manner in which he performs his role in the school social structure. More specifically, the argument entails the following assumptions:

(a) Agents filling the offices of board member, administrator, and teacher in the school structure also occupy positions in the stratification system of the community social structure.

(b) Occupants of positions in the community stratification system internalize the values associated with such positions.

(c) Values relevant to the operation of the school differ from one class stratum to another.

(d) The values which agents of the school internalize by virtue of their class status in the community are the prime determinants of their official acts in the school.

If we accept each of these assumptions, then we can characterize the educative process of the school simply by determining the social class positions of school officials and by describing the educationally-relevant values associated with the positions. Are these assumptions tenable? We shall review each of them briefly, bringing to bear alternative points of view where warranted.

OCCUPANCY OF POSITIONS IN TWO SOCIAL STRUCTURES

To what extent is it possible to view school officers as occupying a position in the social class structure of the community? This is the critical question which we must raise in connection with the first

assumption. In the case of school board members, we have to answer that they are universally an integral part of the community
social structure, and identification of their social class position
within it is a meaningful procedure as long as the community has
a coherent system of stratification. But in the case of the professional
personnel of the school, the answer is not so clear.

In our discussion of the evidence concerning the social status of
administrators, above, we noted certain sociologists abandoned the
attempt to ascribe to administrators a position in the community's
dominant class. Administrators do not typically serve in the schools
of their home communities; more frequently, they are outsiders
brought into a community on a contractual basis. Nor do administrators typically remain in any one community long enough to become a part of it. Many of them fit the description "professional
gypsy." [9] Much of what is written about the teacher's position in the
community applies to the school administrator. A common observation among writers in educational sociology is that teachers are *in*
the community but not *of* the community. Cook, for example, characterizes the teacher as a "stranger" in the community, a person
"detached from the values that bind others" (5, p. 451). Hollingshead makes similar observations about the teachers from outside
Elmtown who form a group apart from the local teachers (8, pp.
129–131). The difficulty the isolation of teachers from the community creates for a social class analysis of school personnel is implied in the following passage:

Assigning social position to teachers on the basis of social participation is
difficult, for, to quote the high school principal, "They don't fit in much
anywhere; they stay pretty much to themselves" (9).

Administrators and particularly teachers are assigned positions in
the social class structure, nevertheless. Two techniques are used,
both of which contain pitfalls. Either the assignment is made within
the class structure of American society at large, rather than within
the community structure, or assignment is made on the basis of their
social class *origins*—the class position of their families. The danger
in the first technique has been pointed out frequently by critics of
the Warner school of social class analysis.[10] Society-wide stratifica-

[9] Karl E. Mosier and John E. Baker, "Midwest Superintendents on the Move,"
Nation's Schools, Vol. 49 (January, 1952), pp. 44–46. These authors present data
for 5700 school superintendents showing clearly the typically short tenure they
hold in any one community.

[10] See, for example, S. M. Lipset and R. Bendix, "Social Status and Social Structure. I," *British Journal of Sociology,* Vol. 2 (June, 1951), pp. 150–168; and "Social
Status and Social Structure."

tion is conceptually an entirely different matter from community stratification, and the two frames of reference cannot be translated into one another indiscriminately. With respect to the second technique, error is bound to occur if one attempts to infer the character of the values and norms to which an adult adheres from information concerning the class position he and his family occupied when he was a child. Although early experience in the social class structure undoubtedly affects the attitudes of an adult, such experience is by no means the sole determinant of his attitudes. To maintain that it is the primary determinant is to overlook the effects of other powerful determinants which may have intervened between childhood and adulthood and the powerful effects of the individual's current social role. We believe this is particularly conducive to error when applied to professional personnel in the school.

If the school community has no coherent social class structure, then it is impossible to locate even school board members within it. It is worth mentioning that contemporary social class theory (at least, the class theory associated with Lloyd Warner) emerged from studies of relatively small, stable, economically independent towns. Towns of this sort are more likely to have a clearly structured system of stratification than metropolitan areas and their dependent suburbia in which the populations are heterogeneous, transient, and lacking in intimate social intercourse. Recent social trends suggest that the small town way of life gradually is passing, and American society is becoming urbanized. The residential population of many school districts can no longer be described meaningfully in terms of its social class structure.[11] The Warner methods simply are not applicable to them. More appropriate for such "communities" are descriptions of power distributions, of special interests, of forces affecting the school originating from outside of the "community" as well as from inside it.

All in all, serious questions arise concerning the adequacy of the first assumption in the argument.

INTERNALIZATION OF CLASS VALUES

The second assumption asserts that a person classified as occupying a particular social class position will internalize the values associ-

---

[11] For a description of the school community relationship in a suburban setting, see Thomas E. Robinson, "The Effects of Suburban Life on Communities and Their Schools," *School Executive*, Vol. 72 (September, 1952), pp. 69–70.

ated with that position. This assumption is a special case of a general problem to which social psychologists have devoted much attention during the last ten or fifteen years, and their research implies that the assumption cannot be accepted until more information is obtained concerning school personnel.

Social psychologists have been confronted by the disturbing fact that persons who are members of a social group according to all the objective criteria one can apply do not always adhere to the values and norms appropriate to their group membership. Some of these persons behave *consistently* in ways foreign to their groups. Close examination of these deviants has shown that many of them, while maintaining membership in their groups, have internalized the values and norms of other groups to which they do not belong. Their behavior is guided by standards of a group other than their membership group.[12]

It is not unreasonable to expect that *some* of the large number of business and professional men whom Counts found on school boards use values and norms other than those of the dominant class to guide their behavior. Similarly, *some* persons of the upper-middle class undoubtedly hold allegiance to the standards of other social classes. In a study of social class affiliations, Centers found marked differences in the attitudes of persons objectively classified in the same social class but who differed in the social class to which they *assigned themselves* (4). If there is a possibility that some persons objectively assigned to a social class position will not reflect the values of their class, we must ascertain whether or not boards are composed of such persons. One might expect that there is a systematic selection of persons for board membership, for example, which eliminates persons with attitudes diverging from those expected of them by virtue of their class position. Or the process of selection may be otherwise: board members may be selected from those "humanitarian" residents of the community who hold a wider set of values than those associated with their own class interests. This is a question of fact which can be answered only by empirical research.

---

[12] The consequence of this research is the now-current distinction between "membership group" and "reference group"—the latter referring to the group which provides the individual with his standards of behavior. He may or may not be a member of his reference group. For an introduction to the theory and research in this area, see Theodore M. Newcomb, *Social Psychology* (New York: Dryden Press, 1950) pp. 220–232; and the four papers constituting Part IV. B., in Guy E. Swanson, T. M. Newcomb, and E. L. Hartley, (Eds.) *Readings in Social Psychology* (New York: Henry Holt and Company, revised, 1952) pp. 410–444.

CLASS DIFFERENCES IN EDUCATIONALLY-RELEVANT VALUES

It is entirely within reason to assume that values relevant to the operation of the school vary from one class stratum to another in the community. At the nation-wide level, opinion surveys consistently find differences in attitudes toward education and the school associated with income level, occupation, and level of education.[13] Community attitude surveys and the sociological community studies further document class differences in educationally-relevant values. One notable finding of many of these studies is that persons in the lower strata of the class structure generally are less critical of the school than those in higher class positions. Does this mean that American schools are *not* reflecting the values of the dominant class to the satisfaction of dominant class members? Other interpretations of the finding seem more defensible, but research is needed to clarify a point so crucial to the argument of the social class analysts.

CLASS VALUES AS DETERMINANTS OF SCHOOL BEHAVIOR

The assumption that the acts of board members, administrators, and teachers are governed *primarily* by the values they bring into the school from their positions in the community social structure is highly questionable. This one-factor interpretation of human behavior is too simplified to account for the complexities observable in the behavior patterns of school officials. If this assumption were true, a person's behavior would be perfectly consistent from one time to another, as long as he maintained the same position in the class structure (or as long as the values associated with his class position remained the same). Moreover, we would find little basic difference in behavior among school officials since they all derive from the same social class. But important differences do exist among school personnel and in the same official from one time to another —differences for which a social class analysis cannot account.

It would be unfair of us to assert that social class analysts accept this assumption. They would admit quickly that other forces are at work to shape human behavior. But the admission that other forces also determine human behavior (or school officials' acts) raises

---

[13] See, for example, National Opinion Research Center, *The Public Looks at Education* (The University of Denver, Denver, Colorado, Report No. 21, August, 1944).

the questions, "What are these forces?" and "How much does each contribute to the determination of behavior in comparison with the social class determinant?" The customary procedure of the social class analysts, particularly in the case study approach, has been to select data concerning the behavior and attitudes of school personnel to *illustrate* the effects of their social class position. The fact that illustrations come to hand is evidence that social class values are *one* determinant of officials' acts. But since no attempt is made to identify and evaluate the effects of other forces, the reader is left with the impression that social class is the major if not the sole determinant of behavior.

Whenever the social class analysts support their argument for dominant class control of the school with observations concerning the class positions of board members, administrators, and teachers, they assume that each of these officers is effective in shaping the educative process of the school. Counts rested his case on observations of board members alone, and, in doing so, assumed implicitly that they are the most powerful agents in determining school affairs. Similarly, those sociologists who view the administrator as an automaton in the service of a dominant class school board are commenting upon the power distribution among school officers and are asserting that administrators typically are powerless *vis-a-vis* the board. The exact nature of the distribution of power in the school has not been the subject of extensive examination, and any assumptions concerning it can only be based upon informal observation or guesswork. The distribution between board and administrator undoubtedly varies from system to system—sometimes the board will exercise tight control over the school, other times the board will acquiesce in large measure to the professional leadership provided by the administrator. In the same way, the degree to which teachers determine the broad outlines as well as the details of the school's educational program probably varies from one school to the next. If the class analysts' argument is to be air-tight, it must incorporate evidence relating to the distribution of power over the educative process among school personnel.

CONCLUSION

In reviewing the assumptions implicit in the argument of dominant class control of the school, we have found reason to question their unqualified applicability to American school systems. Dominant class control has not been demonstrated to the satisfaction of the author; and on dominant class control rests a major share of the proof of the proposition that public schools support the values of the dominant class. But if the assumptions are cast in the form of explicit conditions under which the argument holds, the way is open for empirical investigation of the character of school policy as the conditions vary. In this sense, the social class analysts have laid the foundation for more detailed and yet more comprehensive studies of the school-community interdependence. Moreover, the social class approach to the school embodies a point of view indispensable to a modern analysis of the education system, viz., that the operations of the school and the official acts of its personnel are conditioned importantly by the social setting within which they must function.

As it has developed, the social class approach takes into consideration only certain aspects of the social setting of the school—the stratification system of its community. For this reason its analytical power is severely limited. The independent variable (the social class position of school personnel) is considered to be a constant in our society; and constants can predict only constants. A social theory is needed which can account for the many significant ways in which the educative process of school systems vary from time to time and from community to community. Undoubtedly, some provision for the effects of the community's class structure would be involved in such a theory, but the theory would have to be elaborated extensively and brought into conjunction with theories relating to other forces acting on the school.[14]

[14] The social class analysts proceed from the point of view that class-biased values are brought into the school by school officers; an alternative type of analysis views the school as the focal point of many conflicting pressures which must be resolved by school personnel. School policies result from attempts of the officers to establish a working relationship with an inconsistent and difficult environment; their own values and social position are irrelevant except insofar as they determine the manner in which the conflicts are resolved. Hollingshead tends to rely on this type of analysis. Research from this point of view is concentrated upon the arena of conflict of special interests—the power process—in the community and upon the differential relationships of school personnel *vis-a-vis* the power process. While this approach has not been developed systematically to any appreciable extent, a number of empirical and theoretical studies provide a substantial basis for systematic treatment. Cf., George S. Counts, *School and Society in Chicago* (New York: Harcourt, Brace and Company, 1928); Robert S. Lynd and Helen M. Lynd, *Middletown in Transition* (New York: Harcourt, Brace and Company, 1937); Lloyd A. Cook and Elaine F. Cook, *op. cit.;* and W. B. Spalding, *Public Administration of American Schools* (New York: World Book Company, 1952).

REFERENCES

1. ARNETT, CLAUDE E., *Social Beliefs and Attitudes of School Board Members*. Emporia, Kansas: Emporia Gazette Press, 1932.
2. BROWN, FRANCIS J., *Educational Sociology*. New York: Prentice-Hall, 1947.
3. CAMPBELL, ROALD F., *The Social Implications of School Board Legislation*. Unpublished doctoral thesis. Stanford University, 1942.
4. CENTERS, RICHARD, *The Psychology of Social Classes*. Princeton, N.J.: Princeton University Press, 1949.
5. COOK, LLOYD A., AND ELAINE F. COOK, *A Sociological Approach to Education*. New York: McGraw-Hill, 1950.
6. COUNTS, GEORGE S., The social composition of boards of education: a study in the social control of public education. *Supplementary Educational Monographs*, July, 1927, 33, 83.
7. GARDNER, B. B., M. R. GARDNER, AND M. B. LOEB, Social status and education in a southern community. *School Review*, 1942, 50, 179–191.
8. HOLLINGSHEAD, AUGUST B., *Elmtown's Youth*. New York: John Wiley and Sons, Inc., 1949.
9. JUNKER, B. H., AND M. B. LOEB, The school and social structure in a midwestern community. *School Review*, 1942, 50, 686–695.
10. STEPHENSON, RICHARD, Education and stratification. *Journal of Educational Sociology*, 1951, 25, 1, 37.
11. WARNER, W. LLOYD, *Democracy in Jonesville*. New York: Harper, 1949.
12. WARNER, W. L., R. J. HAVIGHURST, AND M. B. LOEB, *Who Shall Be Educated?* New York: Harper, 1944.

II

The governance of higher education

American higher education is keyed to the economy and social class structure, and this connection is perhaps most starkly apparent in the stratification of students within the college system. Colleges divide and rank students for later entry into a highly hierarchic job market. A student's social class origin has a decisive bearing on the extent and quality of his or her college education, and the type of higher education in turn critically affects the quality of the student's first job. Jerome Karabel's article provides an overview of this process in higher education's lowest track—the community college. He presents data showing that while private universities are predominantly attended by middle and upper-class youth, community colleges draw mainly on working-class and poor youth. Moreover, his evidence indicates that social class tracking continues even within the junior college. Terminal vocational training programs, in contrast to curricula preparing students for transfer to four-year colleges, are filled by those from relatively modest origins. In the end, students are placed in occupations not too different from that of their parents.

Karabel not only describes the basic patterns in community college social class tracking, but also analyzes the political forces behind the adoption of vocational programs. The development of vocational training can be traced both to a business outlook widespread among community college administrators and to overt pressures from the "top." Employers, foundations, the federal government, and associations of college administrators have all pushed for expansion of vocational programs, and their interests have generally prevailed despite widespread student reluctance to enter such programs and occasional outbursts of organized student opposition.

One of the more visible channels of business control of higher education is through their disproportionate representation on college governing boards. The national elite presence on boards of trustees is indeed strong according to Rodney Hartnett's 1968 national survey of more than 5,000 college trustees. Trustees tend to be white, male, Protestant, and Republican—two-thirds identify their own political and social views as close to those of Richard Nixon. Their median income is well over $30,000 and corporate management is the predominant occupation. A business philosophy prevails, and the values of academic freedom do not find great currency.

Yet the governing board is only one of many channels through which capitalist requirements are transmitted into educational practices. Ralph Miliband's selection touches on a variety of other formal and informal means of coordination. One relates to the fact that many college teachers are themselves conservative. Their own deep faith in American capitalism and the political system ensures that the campus curriculum remains within acceptable limits, even without administration and trustee prodding. Intellectual traditions that challenge the academic and political orthodoxy in higher education are viewed with hostility by many teachers. The exclusion is of course far from total, but the overall impact of college instruction remains one of legitimizing the social and economic status quo. However, this socialization is not entirely effective, as Miliband notes, for students are frequently more radical and rebellious in college than before entry. Instruction tends to reinforce confidence and belief in the prevailing social order, but other campus conditions are constantly undermining this faith.

c h a p t e r   s e v e n

Community colleges and social stratification

JEROME KARABEL

In recent years a remarkable transformation has occurred in American higher education, a change as far-ranging in its consequences as the earlier transformation of the American high school from an elite to a mass institution. At the forefront of this development has been the burgeoning two-year community college movement. Enrolling 153,970 students in 1948, two-year public colleges increased their enrollment by one million over the next twenty years to 1,169,635 in 1968 (Department of Health, Education, and Welfare, 1970, p. 75). This growth in enrollment has been accompanied by an increase in the number of institutions; during the 1960's, the number of community colleges increased from 656 to 1,100. Nationally, one-third of all students who enter higher education today start in a community college. In California, the state with the most intricate network of community colleges, students who begin in a community college represent 80 percent of all entering students (Medsker & Tillery, 1971, pp. 16–17). In the future, the role of community colleges in the system of higher education promises to become even larger.

A complex set of forces underlies this extraordinary change in the structure of American higher education. One critical factor in the expansion and differentiation of the system of colleges and universities has been a change in the structure of the economy. Between 1950 and 1970, the proportion of technical and professional workers in

From Jerome Karabel, "Community Colleges and Social Stratification," *Harvard Educational Review*, 42 (November, 1972), pp. 521–30; 540–52; and 555–62. Copyright © 1972 by President and Fellows of Harvard College. Reprinted by permission of the *Harvard Educational Review* and the author.

I would like to thank Christopher Jencks, David Riesman, Russell Thackrey, and Michael Useem for their comments on an earlier draft of this paper. The author takes full responsibility for the views expressed in this article.

the labor force rose from 7.1 percent to 14.5 percent (Bureau of the Census, 1971a, p. 225). Some of this increase took place among traditional professions, such as law and medicine, but much of it occurred among growth fields such as data processing and the health semi-professions which frequently require more than a high school education but less than a bachelor's degree. Community colleges have been important in providing the manpower for this growing middle-level stratum and, if current projections of occupational trends are correct, they are likely to become indispensable in filling labor force needs during the next few years. Openings for library technicians and dental hygienists, for example, jobs for which community colleges provide much of the training, will number 9,000 and 2,400 respectively per year for the next decade. Overall, the largest growth area until 1980 will be the technical and professional category with a projected increase of 50 percent (Bushnell and Zagaris, 1972, p. 135). Without these major changes in the American economy, it is extremely unlikely that the community college movement would have attained its present dimensions.

Although a change in the nature of the labor force laid the groundwork for a system of two-year public colleges, the magnitude and shape of the community college movement owe much to American ideology about equal opportunity through education. Observers, both foreign and domestic, have long noted that Americans take pride in their country's openness—in its apparent capacity to let each person advance as far as his abilities can take him, regardless of social origins. This perceived freedom from caste and class is often contrasted to the aristocratic character of many European societies.[1] America, according to the ideology, is the land of opportunity, and the capstone of its open opportunity structure is its system of public education.

Americans have not only believed in the possibility of upward mobility through education, but have also become convinced that, in a society which places considerable emphasis on credentials, the lack of the proper degrees may well be fatal to the realization of their aspirations. In recent years higher education has obtained a virtual monopoly on entrance to middle and upper level positions in the class structure. Table 1 shows that the probability of holding a high status job, in this case defined as a professional or managerial position, increases sharply with the possession of a bachelor's de-

---

[1] Contrary to popular perceptions, American and European rates of social mobility, at least as measured by mobility from manual to non-manual occupations, are very similar. For data on this point see Lipset and Bendix (1959).

TABLE 1 PERCENTAGE OF U.S. YOUNGER EMPLOYED MALES IN PRO-
FESSIONAL AND MANAGERIAL OCCUPATIONS, BY LEVEL OF EDUCA-
TIONAL ATTAINMENT, LATTER 1960'S

Level of Educational Attainment	Percentage, Professional and Managerial
High school graduation only	7
One or two terms of college	13
Three or four terms of college	28
Five to seven terms of college	32
Eight or more terms of college	82

Source: Unpublished tabulations of the October 1967, 1968, and 1969
Current Population Surveys of the Bureau of the Census, in which the occupations of younger persons, and the imputed earnings for the various occupations were related to levels of educational attainment. (Jaffe and Adams,
1972, p. 249)

gree. This stress on diplomas has led to a clamor for access to higher
education, regardless of social background or past achievements.
The American educational system keeps the mobility "contest" [2]
open for as long as possible and has been willing and able to accom-
modate the demands of the populace for universal access to college.

Response to the pressure for entrance led to greater hierarchical
differentiation within higher education.[3] Existing four-year colleges
did not, for the most part, open up to the masses of students demanding higher education (indeed, selectivity at many of these institutions has increased in recent years); instead, separate two-year
institutions stressing their open and democratic character were created for these new students. Herein lies the genius of the community
college movement: it seemingly fulfills the traditional American
quest for *equality of opportunity* without sacrificing the principle
of *achievement*. On the one hand, the openness of the community
college[4] gives testimony to the American commitment to equality of
opportunity through education; an empirical study by Medsker and

[2] See Ralph Turner's "Modes of Social Ascent through Education" (1966) for a
discussion of how differing norms in the United States and England lead to patterns of "contest" and "sponsored" mobility.

[3] For an empirical study of hierarchical differentiation within higher education,
see "Social Class, Academic Ability and College Quality" by Jerome Karabel and
Alexander W. Astin (American Council on Education, Washington, D.C., forthcoming).

[4] The term "community college" is used in this study to refer to all *public two-
year colleges*. Excluded from this definition are private two-year colleges and all
four-year colleges and universities. In the text, the terms "junior college" and
"two-year college" are used interchangeably with community college though they
are not, strictly speaking, synonyms. The name community college has become

Trent (1965) shows that, among students of high ability and low social status, the rate of college attendance varies from 22 percent in a community with no colleges to 53 percent in a community with a junior college. On the other hand, the community colleges leave the principle of achievement intact by enabling the state colleges and universities to deny access to those citizens who do not meet their qualifications. The latent ideology of the community college movement thus suggests that everyone should have an opportunity to attain elite status, but that once they have had a chance to prove themselves, an unequal distribution of rewards is acceptable. By their ideology, by their position in the implicit tracking system of higher education—indeed, by their very relationship to the larger class structure—the community colleges lend affirmation to the merit principle which, while facilitating individual upward mobility, diverts attention from underlying questions of distributive justice.

The community college movement is part of a larger historical process of educational expansion. In the early twentieth century, the key point of expansion was at the secondary level as the high school underwent a transition from an elite to a mass institution. Then, as now, access to education was markedly influenced by socioeconomic status.[5]

As the high school became a mass institution, it underwent an internal transformation (Trow, 1966). Formerly providing uniform training to a small group of relatively homogeneous students in order to enable them to fill new white-collar jobs, the high school responded to the massive influx of students by developing a differentiated curriculum. The main thrust of this new curriculum was to provide terminal rather than college preparatory education.

Martin Trow places this "first transformation of American sec-

---

the more frequently used because of the increasing emphasis of two-year public institutions on fulfilling local needs. Further, as the community college struggled to obtain a distinct identity and as greater stress was placed on two-year programs, the junior college label, which seemingly describes a lesser version of the four-year college geared almost exclusively to transfer, became increasingly inappropriate.

[5] Two of the most comprehensive recent studies of the influence of social class and ability on access to higher education are Sewell and Shah (1967) and Folger *et al.* (1970). George Counts (1922: 149), in a classical empirical study of the American high school of a half century ago, concluded that "in very large measure participation in the privilege of a secondary education is contingent on social and economic status." Similarly, Michael Katz (1968), in a study of public education reform in nineteenth century Massachusetts, found that the early high school was overwhelmingly a middle class institution.

ondary education" between 1910 and 1940. During this period, the proportion of the 14 to 17 age group attending rose from about 15 percent to over 70 percent. Since World War II, a similar transformation has been taking place in American higher education: in 1945, 16.3 percent of the 18 to 21 age group was enrolled in college; by 1968, the proportion had grown to 40.8 percent (Department of Health, Education and Welfare, 1970, p. 67). This growth has been accompanied by increasing differentiation in higher education, with the community colleges playing a pivotal role in this new division of labor. In short, educational expansion seems to lead to some form of tracking which, in turn, distributes people in a manner which is roughly commensurate with both their class origins and their occupational destination.

The process by which the educational system expands without narrowing relative differences between groups or changing the underlying opportunity structure may be referred to as "educational inflation" (cf. Milner, 1972). Like economic inflation, educational inflation means that what used to be quite valuable (e.g., a high diploma) is worth less than it once was. As lower socioeconomic groups attain access to a specific level of education, educational escalation is pushed one step higher. When the high school was democratized, sorting continued to take place through the mechanism of tracking, with higher status children taking college preparatory programs and lower status children enrolling in terminal vocational courses; similarly as access to college was universalized, the allocative function continued to occur through the provision of separate schools, two-year community colleges, which would provide an education for most students that would not only be different from a bachelor's degree program, but also shorter. The net effect of educational inflation is thus to vitiate the social impact of extending educational opportunity to a higher level.

If the theory of educational inflation is correct, we would expect that the tremendous expansion of the educational system in the twentieth century has been accompanied by minimal changes in the system of social stratification. Indeed, various studies indicate that the rate of social mobility has remained fairly constant in the last half-century (Lipset and Bendix, 1959; Blau and Duncan, 1967) as has the distribution of wealth and income (Kolko, 1962; Miller, 1971; Jencks, 1972). Apparently, the extension of educational opportunity, however much it may have contributed to other spheres such as economic productivity and the general cultural level of the society, has resulted in little or no change in the overall extent of social mobility and economic inequality. . . .

THE COMPOSITION OF THE
COMMUNITY COLLEGE
STUDENT BODY

If community colleges occupy the bottom of a tracking system within higher education that is closely linked to the external class structure, the social composition of the two-year public college should be proportionately lower in status than that of more prestigious four-year institutions. Christopher Jencks and David Riesman, in *The Academic Revolution* (1968, p. 485), however, citing 1966 American Council on Education data, suggest that the "parents of students who enroll at community colleges are slightly *richer* than the parents of students at four-year institutions." This conclusion is derived from the small income superiority students at two-year public colleges had over students at four-year public colleges in 1966; it ignores public universities and all private institutions. Several other studies, most of them more recent, show that community college students *do* come from lower-class backgrounds, as measured by income, occupation, and education, than do their counterparts at four-year colleges and universities (Medsker and Trent, 1965; Schoenfeldt, 1968; American Council on Education, 1971; Medsker and Tillery, 1971; Bureau of the Census, 1972).

TABLE 2   FATHER'S OCCUPATIONAL CLASSIFICATION BY TYPE OF COLLEGE ENTERED (PERCENTAGES)

	Father's Occupational Classification			
Type of College	Skilled, Semi-skilled, Unskilled	Semi-professional, Small Business, Sales and Clerical	Professional and Managerial	Total
Public two-year	55	29	16	100
Public four-year	49	32	19	100
Private four-year	38	30	32	100
Public university	32	33	35	100
Private university	20	31	49	100

Source: Medsker and Trent (1965)

Table 2 presents data showing the distribution of fathers' occupations at various types of colleges. Community colleges are lowest in terms of social class; they have the fewest children of professionals and managers (16 percent) and the most of blue-collar workers (55 percent). Private universities, the most prestigious of the categories and the one linked most closely to graduate and professional schools, have the highest social composition: 49 percent professional and managerial and only 20 percent blue-collar. Interestingly, the proportion of middle-level occupations shows little variation among the various types of colleges.

Having demonstrated the lower-middle and working-class character of community colleges, it would seem to follow that college type is also related to family income. Table 3, based on nationally rep-

TABLE 3   FAMILY INCOME BY TYPE OF COLLEGE ENTERED (PERCENTAGES)

Type of College	Family Income				
	Under $8,000	$8,000–12,499	$12,500–20,000	Over $20,000	Total
Public two-year	27.2	34.8	26.4	11.5	100
Public four-year	25.4	31.7	28.3	14.7	100
Public university	15.1	29.7	32.8	22.3	100
Private university	10.6	20.4	27.3	41.8	100

Source: American Council on Education (1971, p. 39)

resentative American Council on Education data for 1971, reveals systematic income differences among the student bodies at various types of colleges. Over one-quarter of all community college students are from relatively low income families (under $8,000) compared with about 11 percent at private universities. Affluent students (over $20,000) comprise 12 percent of the student body at community colleges but over 40 percent at private institutions. The four-year public colleges show income distributions between community colleges and private universities.

Prestige differences among colleges also correspond to differences in fathers' educational attainment. In Table 4, American Council

TABLE 4   FATHER'S EDUCATION BY TYPE OF COLLEGE ENTERED (PERCENTAGES)

Type of College	Father's Education						
	Grammar School or Less	Some High School	High School Graduate	Some College	College Graduate	Post-graduate Degree	Total
Public two-year	12.7	21.3	31.7	19.1	11.5	3.8	100
Public four-year	12.1	19.4	34.7	17.9	11.1	4.8	100
Public university	8.0	13.9	29.0	20.3	19.0	9.8	100
Private university	4.6	9.6	21.9	18.9	24.4	20.5	100
Elite[a]	1.2	3.5	10.6	13.1	31.3	40.5	100

[a] Elite colleges are defined as institutions having average freshman SAT's over 650. For more data on elite colleges see Karabel and Astin (forthcoming).

Source: American Council on Education (1967, p. 22)

on Education data for 1966 show that the proportion of students whose fathers graduated from college ranges from 15 percent at community colleges to 72.6 percent at elite institutions (colleges with average Scholastic Aptitude Tests over 650). Over one third of public two-year college students have fathers who did not graduate from high school compared with less than 5 percent at elite colleges.

The data on occupation, income, and education all run in the same direction and testify to an increase in social class position as one ascends the prestige hierarchy of colleges and universities. Community colleges, at the bottom of the tracking system in higher education, are also lowest in student body class composition. That college prestige is a rough indicator of factors leading to adult occupational attainment and of adult socioeconomic status itself is borne out by a number of studies (Havemann and West, 1952; Reed and Miller, 1970; Wolfle, 1971; Pierson, 1969; Collins, 1971; Spaeth, 1968; Sharp, 1970; Folger *et al.*, 1970). Thus, the current tracking system in higher education may help transmit inequality intergenerationally. Lower class students disproportionately attend community colleges which, in turn, channel them into relatively low status jobs.

However related attendance at a community college may be to social origins, students are not explicitly sorted into the hierarchically differentiated system of higher education on the basis of social class. More important than class background in predicting where one goes to college is measured academic ability (Folger *et al.*, 1970, pp. 166–167; Karabel and Astin, forthcoming). Schoenfeldt (1968), using Project TALENT data, reports that junior college students are more like noncollege students in terms of academic ability and more like four-year college students in terms of socioeconomic status. A review of research on the ability of junior college students by Cross (1968) concludes that they show substantially less measured academic ability than their four-year counterparts although there is a great diversity in academic ability *among* junior college students. In a sample of 1966 high school graduates in four states who entered community colleges, 19 percent were in the highest quartile of academic ability (Medsker & Tillery, 1971, p. 38). As is common with aggregate data, generalizations obscure important variations among individuals. In California, where admission to the state colleges and university are limited to the top $33\frac{1}{3}$ and $12\frac{1}{2}$ percent in ability respectively, approximately 26 and 6 percent of students who choose a junior college would have been eligible for a state college or university (Coordinating Council, 1969, p. 79).

There is evidence that many high ability students who attend community colleges are of modest social origins. In California, for example, the proportion of eligible students who choose to attend the state colleges or university varies from 22.5 percent among students from families with incomes of under $4,000 to over 50 percent in the $20,000–25,000 category (Hansen and Weisbrod, 1969, p. 74). It is assumed that many of these low-income students attend a nearby two-year college. Table 5 estimates the probability of a male

TABLE 5   PROBABILITY OF A MALE ENTERING A TWO-YEAR COLLEGE

Socioeconomic Quarter	Ability Quarter			
	Low 1	2	3	High 4
Low 1	.04	.07	.06	.16
2	.03	.07	.10	.08
3	.07	.11	.10	.08
High 4	.11	.12	.11	.05

Source: Schoenfeldt (1968, p. 357)

student entering a junior college (public and private). The likeliest entrant at a two-year college is the person of high academic ability and low social status followed by the high status student of less than average ability. These data, however, cannot be construed as providing the relative proportion of intelligent, poor students as opposed to mediocre, rich students in the community college; instead, they merely show the probability of attending a two-year college *if* someone falls into a particular category. Table 5 also illustrates that there is a diversity of both social class and academic ability in the community college. Internal diversity notwithstanding, the community college does indeed stand at the bottom of the tracking system in higher education not only from the perspective of social class, but also from that of academic ability. . . .

TRACKING WITHIN THE COMMUNITY COLLEGE— VOCATIONAL EDUCATION

The subordinate position of the community college within the tracking system of higher education has often been noted. What has been less frequently noted is that tracking also takes place *within* the community college. Two-year public colleges are almost always open door institutions, but admission to programs within them is often on a selective basis. What this generally means in practice is that students who are not "transfer material" are either tracked into vocational programs or cooled out altogether.*

Class-based tracking, whether between schools, within schools, or both, is not new in American education. This pattern extends back into the early twentieth century, the period during which the American high school became a mass institution.⁶ If the theory of class-based hierarchical differentiation in education is applied to the question of tracking within the community college, it would lead us to expect a relatively low class composition among students in vocational programs.

Data presented in Table 6 show a pronounced class bias in the composition of community college students enrolled in vocational programs. Compared with students in transfer programs, vocational students are markedly lower in family income, father's education, and father's occupation. While almost half of community college students in the transfer curriculum are from white-collar families, only one-fourth of the students in vocational programs are from such backgrounds. Students enrolled in technical programs fall in between vocational and transfer students along various measures of socioeconomic status. Black students show themselves to be considerably more likely than white students to enroll in community college vocational programs.⁷

* [Editor's note: "Cooling out" refers to a process described by Burton Clark (1960) in which community college students who want to transfer to a four-year college but who would probably fail in such efforts are subtly persuaded to abandon these aspirations.]

⁶ When George L. Counts examined class differences in secondary schools in the early twenties, he wrote:

> These differences in the extent of educational opportunity are further accentuated through the choice of curricula. As a rule, those groups which are poorly represented in the high school patronize the more narrow and practical curricula, the curricula which stand as terminal points in the educational system and which prepare for wage-earning. And the poorer their representation in high school, the greater is the probability that they will enter these curricula. The one- and two-year vocational courses, wherever offered, draw their registration particularly, from the ranks of labor (Counts, 1922, p. 143). See also Trow, 1966; Cohen and Lazerson, 1972; Greer, 1972.

⁷ Minority students are also disproportionately enrolled in two of the lower rungs of the higher education tracking system—community colleges and unselective black colleges. Patterns of enrollment, of course, vary from region to region with community colleges dominant in the West and black institutions more prominent in the South. For data showing that the proportion of minority students decreases as one progresses up the three-track California system see Coordinating Council (1969: 23) and Jaffe and Adams (1972: 232).

TABLE 6 SELECTED CHARACTERISTICS OF STUDENTS ENROLLED IN THREE CURRICULUMS IN 63 COMPREHENSIVE COMMUNITY COLLEGES (PERCENTAGES)

Characteristics	College Parallel	Technical	Vocational
Father's occupation			
Unskilled or semiskilled	18	26	35
White collar	46	35	25
Parental Income			
Less than $6,000	14	14	24
More than $10,000	36	28	21
Father's formal education			
Less than high school graduation	27	34	50
Some college or more	31	20	14
Race			
Caucasian	91	79	70
Negro	5	7	14
Oriental	1	7	7
Other	1	4	6

Source: Comparative Guidance and Placement Program, 1969. (Cross, 1970, p. 191)

The relatively low social origins of vocational and technical students are likely to be reflected in their adult occupations. Community college occupational programs are broadly designed to prepare people for entrance into the growing technical and semi-professional stratum. Estimates as to the size of this expanding class suggest that it may comprise one-third of the labor force by 1975 (Harris, 1971, p. 254). This stratum occupies the lower-middle levels of the system of social stratification, but it creates a sensation of upward mobility among its members because it is representative of the change from a blue-collar (or secondary) to a white-collar (or tertiary) economy. Since many members of this "new working class" originate from blue-collar backgrounds, their movement into this stratum does in fact represent mobility. Yet it may be conjectured that this perception of mobility is only temporary: as more and more people move into these jobs, the prestige of a white-collar position may undergo a corresponding decline in status.[8]

[8] At the same time, however, it is easy to forget that *absolute* changes in occupation, income, and educational attainment can have important consequences in everyday life and may raise general levels of satisfaction. Having more people attend college, while not narrowing the educational gap in relative terms, may lead to a more enlightened populace. Keniston and Gerzon (1972) attack the narrowly economic view of higher education and argue that important non-pecuniary

Evidence on the economic returns of these vocational programs is, at best, indirect, and empirical studies on this topic would be extremely useful. Yet it is apparent that, in general, having two years of college is not half as good as having four years (Bowles, 1971, Jaffe & Adams, 1972). Table 7, based on recent Census Bureau data,

TABLE 7   YEARLY INCOME OF U.S. YOUNGER EMPLOYED MALES, BY LEVEL OF EDUCATIONAL ATTAINMENT, LATE 1960S (BASE: HIGH SCHOOL GRADUATION INCOME = 100)

Level of Educational Attainment	Income	Percentage of All College Dropouts
High school graduation	100	—
One or two terms of college	110	40
Three or four terms of college	119	37
Five to seven terms of college	121	23
Eight or more terms of college	150	—

Source: Unpublished tabulations of the October 1967, 1968, and 1969 Current Population Surveys of the Bureau of the Census, in which the occupations of younger persons, and the imputed earnings for the various occupations were related to levels of educational attainment. (Jaffe and Adams, 1972, p. 249)

indicates that the recipient of five to seven terms of college is closer in income to a high school graduate than to a college graduate. Possibly, there is some sort of "sheepskin effect" associated with the attainment of a bachelor's degree. But whatever the reasons, having part of a college education seems to be of limited economic value. Whether this is also true for community college students in programs specially designed to prepare them for an occupation remains to be seen.[9]

---

benefits accrue from college attendance. Similarly, a change from a blue-collar to a white-collar economy may eliminate many menial tasks and hence lead to a greater job satisfaction. Finally, an absolute increase in the standard of living, while not necessarily abolishing poverty (which, as Jencks argues, is primarily a relative phenomenon), may result in a higher quality of life than was possible under conditions of greater scarcity.

[9] Lazerson and Grubb (1973) report that economic returns to vocational education are almost uniformly low, but their review does not include studies of programs at community colleges. Some skepticism as to the allegedly high incomes of graduates of occupational programs for blue-collar jobs may, however, be expressed. Contrary to popular mythology about the affluent worker, the proportion of male blue-collar workers earning more than $15,000 in 1970 was a miniscule 4 percent (Bureau of the Census, 1971b: 30). Only 3 out of 10 blue-collar workers earned more than $10,000 in 1970.

We do not know what economic rewards accrue to graduates of community college vocational programs, nor do we know much about the occupational and

THE SPONSORS OF THE VOCATIONAL MOVEMENT

Unlike the movement for open admissions to college, which received much of its impetus from mass pressure, there has been little popular clamor for community college vocational programs. Indeed, most junior college entrants see the two-year college as a way-station to a four-year college and shun occupational programs (see the next section). Despite this, there has been an enormous push to increase enrollment in community college occupational programs. This push from the top for more career education marks one of the major developments in the evolution of the community college movement.

The interest of the business community in encouraging occupational training at public expense is manifest. With a changing labor force which requires ever increasing amounts of skill to perform its tasks and with manpower shortages in certain critical areas, private industry is anxious to use the community college as a training ground for its employees. An associate of the Space Division of the North American Rockwell Corporation makes the corporate viewpoint clear: "industry . . . must recognize that junior colleges are indispensible to the fulfillment of its needs for technical manpower" (Ryan, 1971, p. 71). In the Los Angeles area, Space Division personnel and junior college faculty work together to set up curricular requirements, frame course content, determine student competence, and formulate "on-the-job performance objectives."

The influence of the business community on the junior college is exerted in part through membership of local industrial notables on community college boards of trustees. Hartnett (1969, p. 28) reports that 33 percent of public junior college trustees are business executives and that over half of all community college trustees agree that "running a college is basically like running a business." Overt business interference in the affairs of the community college is, however, probably rare; the ideological influence of the business community, with its emphasis on pragmatism and economic efficiency, is so pervasive in the two-year college that conflicts between the industrial and educational communities would not normally arise. One imagines that Arthur M. Cohen (1971b, p. 6), Director of the ERIC

---

economic status of the community college drop-out. This is fertile ground for empirical inquiry. A longitudinal study of three groups of high school graduates —students who do not enter college, community college drop-outs, and community college entrants who obtain a degree (A.A. or B.A.)—matching students with similar personal characteristics, would do much to illuminate the effects of attending a community college.

Clearinghouse for Junior Colleges, is hardly exaggerating when he says that when "corporate managers . . . announce a need for skilled workers, . . . college administrators trip over each other in their haste to organize a new technical curriculum."

Foundations have also shown an intense interest in junior college vocational programs, an interest which is somewhat more difficult to explain than that of business and industry. The Kellogg Foundation, which over a period of years, has made grants to the community college movement totaling several million dollars (Gleazer, 1968, p. 38), has a long-standing interest in career training. In 1959, the general director of the Kellogg Foundation noted approvingly that the "community college movement can do much to supply the sub-professionals, the technicians so necessary to the professions and industry in the years ahead" (Powell, 1965, p. 17). Kellogg followed up on this interest in career education with grants to Chicago City Junior College in 1963 and 1964 for associate degree programs in nursing and business which came to $312,440 and $112,493 respectively (Sunko, 1965, p. 42). In addition, in the late 1950's, Kellogg made a several hundred thousand dollar commitment to support the American Association of Junior Colleges, the national organization of the two-year college movement which has itself been a long-time advocate of vocational programs (Brick, 1964).

The Carnegie Commission on Higher Education, financially sponsored by, but independent of, the Carnegie Corporation of New York, has also been active in sponsoring career education. In its widely read pamphlet, *The Open-Door Colleges,* the Carnegie Commission (1970), made explicit policy proposals for community colleges. Members of the Commission came out strongly for occupational programs, and stated that they "should be given the fullest support and status within community colleges" and should be "flexibly geared to the changing requirements of society" (1970, p. 1). Later in the report (pp. 15–16) the Commission recommended that community colleges remain two-year institutions lest they "place less emphasis on occupational programs." Community colleges, the Commission said, "should follow an open-enrollment policy, whereas access to four-year institutions should generally be more selective." The net impact of these recommendations is to leave the tracking system of higher education intact. Considering the class composition of the community college, to maintain the status quo in higher education tracking is, in essence, to perpetuate privilege (see Wolfe, 1971).

The influence of foundations in fostering vocational education in community colleges is difficult to measure precisely, but it is clear that they have been among its leading sponsors.[10] State master plans (see Hurlburt, 1969; Cross, 1970) have also done much to formalize the subordinate status of the community college within higher education and to encourage the growth of their vocational curricula. The federal government, too, has promoted vocational training in the two-year institutions. Federal involvement dates back at least to 1963. At that time, Congress authorized the spending of several hundred million dollars to encourage post-secondary technical education. More recently, the Higher Education Act of 1972 (pp. 77–78) authorized $850,000,000 over the next three years for post-secondary occupational education. In comparison, the entire sum authorized for the establishment of new community colleges and the expansion of old ones is less than one-third as much—$275,000,000.

The language of the Higher Education Act of 1972 makes clear just what is meant by vocational education:

The term "postsecondary occupational education" means education, training, or retraining . . . conducted by an institution . . . which is designed to prepare individuals for gainful employment as semi-skilled or skilled workers or technicians or sub-professionals in recognized occupations (including new and emerging occupations) . . . but excluding any program to prepare individuals for employment in occupations . . . to be generally considered professional or which require a baccalaureate or advanced degree. (p. 87)

The import of this definition of occupational education is to exclude four-year programs leading to a B.A. from funding. The intent of this legislation, which provides enormous sums of money for community college career education, is obvious: it is designed to fill current manpower shortage in the middle and lower-middle levels of the occupational structure.

The idea of career education which the U.S. Office of Education is "working to spread throughout elementary, secondary and at least community college circles" (Marland, 1972, p. 217) is that the student, regardless of when he leaves the educational system, should have sufficient skills to enable him to be gainfully employed. The idea is a worthy one, but it implicitly accepts the existing system of social stratification. The philosophy of career education is that the proper function of the educational system is to respond to current

---

[10] Karier (1972) has written a provocative essay on the role of foundations in sponsoring educational testing. The role of far-sighted foundations in fostering educational reform, possibly as a means of rationalizing the social order, is a topic worthy of careful investigation.

manpower needs and to allocate people to positions characterized by large disparities in rewards. Commissioner of Education, Sidney Marland, observes that no more than 20 percent of all jobs in the 1970's will require a bachelor's degree; apparently, this is supposed to provide a rough index as to how many people should attend college for four years. Further, it is worth noting that career education does not seem to extend above the community college level. An idea whose "time has come," it somehow does not seem applicable to the sons and daughters of the middle and upper classes who attend four-year colleges and universities.

Federal sponsorship of vocational programs in the community college may have contributed to the development of a rigid track system (Cohen, 1971a, p. 152). By prohibiting the allocation of funds to non-vocational programs, federal laws have deepened the division between transfer and occupational programs. This division fosters separate facilities, separate brochures, and separate administrations. The result is a magnification of the differences between transfer and vocational programs leading to a decline in the desirability of occupational training.

Also at the forefront of the movement to expand vocational programs in community colleges have been various national higher education organizations. The American Association of Junior Colleges (AAJC), almost since its founding in 1920, has exerted its influence to encourage the growth of vocational education. Faced with the initial problem of establishing an identity for two-year colleges, the AAJC set out to describe the unique functions of the junior college. Prominent among these was the provision of two-year occupational training at the post-secondary level. In 1940 and 1941 the AAJC sponsored a Commission on Junior College Terminal Education. According to Ralph Fields (1962), a long-time observer of the junior college, this commission was instrumental in lending legitimacy to vocational training in the community college.

In recent years, the AAJC has continued its active encouragement of occupational programs in the community college. Numerous pamphlets, training programs, and conferences on vocational training in the two-year college have been sponsored by AAJC. In that the AAJC, the leading national association of junior colleges, has probably done more than any other single organization to give definition to the community college movement, its enthusiasm for vocational training takes on particular importance.

The American Council on Education, the umbrella organization for the various associations of higher education, is considered by many to be the leading spokesman for American higher education. It, too, has given major support to post-secondary technical education. In 1963, the Council sponsored a study of the place of technical and vocational training in higher education. One of the conclusions of the report was that "two-year colleges, if they are to assume their proper and effective role in the educational system of the nation, should make vocational and technical education programs a major part of their mission and a fundamental institutional objective" (Venn, 1964, p. 165). Edmund Gleazer, Jr. (1968, p. 139), Executive Director of AAJC, points to this report as critical in gaining acceptance for vocational training within the higher education community.

Finally, many American universities have looked with favor on the development of the community college into a "comprehensive" institution with occupational programs in addition to its more traditional transfer programs. From the origins of the junior college in the late nineteenth and early twentieth centuries as an institution designed to extend secondary education for two years in order to keep the university pure, there has been a recognition among many university academics that it is in their interest to have a diversity of institutions in higher education (Thornton, 1960, pp. 46–50). A number of observers have noted that the community colleges serve as a safety valve, diverting students clamoring for access to college away from more selective institutions (Clark, 1960; Jencks and Riesman, 1968; Cohen, 1971b). Elite colleges neither want nor need these students; if separate institutions, or, for that matter, vocational programs within these institutions help keep the masses out of their colleges, then they are to be given full support.[11] Paradoxically, the elite sector of the academic community, much of it liberal to radical, finds itself in a peculiar alliance with industry, foundations, government, and established higher education associations to vocationalize the community college.[12]

[11] Amitai Etzioni (1970), chairman of the Department of Sociology at Columbia University, expresses this point of view well: "If we can no longer keep the floodgates closed at the admissions office, it at least seems wise to channel the general flow away from four-year colleges and toward two-year extensions of high school in the junior and community colleges." Vice President Agnew (1970), in a speech attacking open admissions, approvingly cited this quotation.

[12] See Riessman's "The 'Vocationalization' of Higher Education: Duping the Poor" for an analysis of the movement to turn the community college into a technical institution. For a brilliant article on the elitism of leftist academics toward working-class students see McDermott (1969).

THE RESPONSE TO VOCATIONAL EDUCATION:
SUBMERGED CLASS CONFLICT

Despite the massive effort by leading national educational policy-makers to encourage the development of occupational education in the community college, student response to vocational programs has been limited. Estimates vary as to how many community college students are enrolled in career education programs, but the figures seem to range from 25 to 33 percent (Cross, 1970; Ogilvie, 1971; Medsker and Tillery, 1971). Over two-thirds of two-year college entrants aspire to a bachelor's degree, and a similar proportion enroll, at least initially, in college-parallel or transfer programs. Many of these students, of course, are subsequently cooled out, but few of them seem to prefer a vocational program to leaving the community college altogether.

Leaders of the occupational education movement have constantly bemoaned the lack of student enthusiasm for vocational education (Venn, 1964; Gleazer, 1968; Carnegie, 1970; Medsker and Tillery, 1971; Cross, 1971). The problem, they believe, is the low status of career training in a society that worships the bachelor's degree. Medsker and Tillery (p. 140), for example, argue that "negative attitudes toward vocational education . . . are by-products of the academic syndrome in American higher education." Marland (1972, p. 218) refers to the difficulty as "degree fixation." The problem, then, since it is one of an irrational preoccupation with obtaining a traditional four-year education, leads to an obvious solution: raising the status of vocational education. This proposed solution has been suggested by the Carnegie Commission on Higher Education, the Office of Education, the American Association of Junior Colleges, the American Council on Education, leaders of industry, and scholars in the field of community colleges.

Despite the apparent logic and simplicity of raising the status of vocational education, the task presents enormous difficulties. Minority students, though more likely to be enrolled in occupational programs than white students, seem especially sensitive to being channeled into vocational tracks. Overall, students are voting with their feet against community college vocational programs.

This is not an irrational obsession with four-year diplomas on the part of the students. It is not just snobbish prejudice; there are sound structural reasons for the low status of career education in the community college. At the base of an educational institution's prestige is its relationship to the occupational and class structure of the society in which it operates (Clark, 1962, pp. 80–83). The community college lies at the base of the stratification structure of higher education both in the class origins of its students and in their occupational destinations. Within the community college, the vocational curriculum is at the bottom of the prestige hierarchy—again, both in terms of social composition and likely adult status.

It is unrealistic, then, to expect that community college vocational programs, the bottom track of higher education's bottom track, will have much status. It is worth noting that the British, generally more hardheaded about matters of social class than Americans, faced the matter of educational status directly some years ago. In the 1950's in Great Britain, there was a great deal of talk about "parity of esteem" in English secondary education. The problem was to give equal status to grammar schools (college preparatory), technical schools (middle level managerial and technical), and secondary modern schools (terminal). After considerable debate, the British realized that "parity of esteem" was an impossible ideal given the encompassing class structure (Banks, 1955; Marshall, 1965).

The educational establishment's concern with the low status of occupational programs in the community colleges reveals much more about its own ideology than it does about the allegedly irrational behavior of students resistant to vocational education. A great deal of emphasis is placed on improving the public image of vocational education, but little attention is paid to the substantive matter of class differences in income, occupational prestige, power, and opportunities for autonomy and expression at the workplace. The Carnegie Commission, whose ideology is probably representative of the higher education establishment, blurs the distinction between *equality* and *equality of opportunity* (Karabel, 1972a, p. 42). Discussing its vision of the day when minority persons will be proportionately represented in higher occupational levels, the Commission hails this as an "important signal that society was meeting its commitment to equality." The conception of equality conveyed in this passage is really one of equality of opportunity; the Commission seems less interested in reducing gross differences in rewards than in giving everyone a chance to get ahead of everyone else. The Carnegie Commission, reflecting the values not only of the national educational leadership but also of the wider society, shows concern about opportunities for mobility, but little concern about a reduction in inequality.

The submerged class conflict that exists between the sponsors of vocational education in the junior college, who represent the interests and outlook of the more privileged sectors of society, and com-

munity college students, many of them working class, occasionally
becomes overt. At Seattle Community College in 1968–1969, the
Black Student Union vigorously opposed a recommendation to con-
centrate trade and technical programs in the central (Black) campus
while the "higher" semiprofessional programs were allocated to the
northern and southern (white) campuses (Cohen, 1971a: 142). Rutgers (Newark) was the scene in 1969 of extensive demonstrations to
gain open admissions to a branch of the state university. The import
of the case of Rutgers (Newark) was that the protests took place in
a city where students already had access to an open-door community
college (Essex) and a mildly selective state college (Newark State).
What the students were resisting here was not being tracked within
the community college, but rather being channeled into the community college itself.[13] The well-known struggle for open admissions
at CUNY in the spring of 1969 was not primarily for access per se,
but for access to the more prestigious four-year institutions: City,
Brooklyn, Queens, and Hunter.

The pattern in these isolated cases of manifest resistance to tracking within or between colleges is one of minority student leadership.
In the United States, where race is a much more visible social cleav-
age than class, it is not surprising that Black students have shown
the most sensitivity to tracking in higher education. Channeling of
Black students to community colleges and to vocational programs
within them is, after all, fairly visible; in contrast, the *class* character of the tracking system is much less perceptible. Were it not for
the militancy of some minority students, it is likely that the conflict over vocational education would have long continued to manifest itself in enrollment patterns without becoming overt.

The class nature of the conflict over tracking has, however, not
always been invisible. In Illinois in 1913, there was a battle over a
bill in the state legislature to establish a separate system of vocational schools above the sixth grade. Business strongly backed the
bill, sponsored by Chicago School Superintendent Edwin G. Cooley.
The Chicago Federation of Labor, lobbying against the bill, expressed fear that it reflected

an effort on the part of large employers to turn the public schools into an
agency for supplying them with an adequate supply of docile, well-trained,
and capable workers [which] . . . aimed to bring Illinois a caste system of
education which would shunt the children of the laboring classes at an
early age first into vocational courses and then into the factories (Counts,
1928, p. 167).

[13] I am indebted to Russell Thackrey for pointing out the implications of the
interesting case of Rutgers (Newark).

After a bitter fight, the bill was defeated in the legislature.

The tracking which takes place in the community college is, however, much more invisible than that proposed in the Cooley Bill. For one thing, the community college, by the very use of the word "college" in its title, locates itself squarely within the system of higher education and gives it at least the minimal status which comes from being a college rather than a technical school. For another, the apparent emphasis of the junior college on the transfer function leads to a perception of it as a way station on the road to a four-year college. This view of the community college as a place of transfer rather than a track is strengthened by the subtlety and smoothness of the cooling out process. The community college is a "comprehensive" institution; like the high school before it, it provides preparatory and terminal education in the same building and offers sufficient opportunities for movement between programs to obscure the larger pattern of tracking. Finally, the very age at which students enter the community college makes tracking a less serious issue; there *is* a difference between channeling an eleven-year-old child and channeling a young adult of eighteen.

Whatever the differences between high school and college tracking, there is a marked similarity in the rationales given in each case for curricular differentiation. The argument is that a common curriculum denies equality of opportunity by restricting educational achievement to a single mode which will inevitably lead to some form of hierarchy. In 1908, the Boston school superintendent argued:

> Until very recently [the schools] have offered equal opportunity to receive *one kind* of education, but what will make them democratic is to provide opportunity for all to receive such an education as will fit them *equally well* for their particular life work. (Cohen and Lazerson, 1972: 69)

Similarly, K. Patricia Cross (1971: 162), a leading researcher on the junior college, argues more than 60 years later:

> Surely quality education consists not in offering the same thing to all people in a token gesture toward equality but in maximizing the match between the talents of the individual and the teaching resources of the institution. Educational quality is not uni-dimensional. Colleges can be *different* and excellent too.

In principle, colleges can be different and excellent, too. But in a stratified society, what this diversity of educational experiences is likely to mean is that people will, at best, have an equal opportunity to obtain an education that will fit them into their appropriate position in the class structure. More often than not, those of lower class origins will, under the new definition of equality of educational opportunity, find themselves in schools or curricula which train them for positions roughly commensurate with their social origins.

The current movement to vocationalize the community college is a logical outgrowth of the dual historical patterns of class-based hierarchical differentiation in education and of educational inflation. The system of higher education, forced to respond to pressure for access arising from mobility aspirations endemic in an affluent society which stresses individual success and the democratic character of its opportunity structure, has let people in and has then proceeded to track them into community colleges and, more particularly, into occupational programs within these two-year colleges. This push toward vocational training in the community college has been sponsored by a national educational planning elite whose social composition, outlook, and policy proposals are reflective of the interests of the more privileged strata of our society. Notably absent among those pressuring for more occupational training in the junior college have been the students themselves. . . .

DISCUSSION

The recent Newman Report on Higher Education (1971: 57) noted that "the public, and especially the four-year colleges and universities, are shifting more and more responsibility onto the community colleges for undertaking the toughest tasks of higher education." One of the most difficult of these tasks has been to educate hundreds of thousands of students, many of them of modest social origins, in whom more selective colleges and universities showed no interest. Community colleges have given these students access to higher education and have provided some of them a chance to advance their class position.

Despite the idealism and vigor of the community college movement, there has been a sharp contradiction between official rhetoric and social reality. Hailed as the "democratizers of higher education," community colleges are, in reality, a vital component of the class-based tracking system. The modal junior college student, though aspiring to a four-year diploma upon entrance, receives neither an associate nor a bachelor's degree. The likelihood of his persisting in higher education is *negatively* influenced by attending a community college. Since a disproportionate number of two-year college students are of working-class origins, low status students are most likely to attend those institutions which increase the likelihood that they will drop out of college. Having increased access to higher education, community colleges are notably unsuccessful in retaining their students and in reducing class differentials in educational opportunity.

If current trends continue, the tracking system of higher education may well become more rigid. The community college, as the bottom track, is likely to absorb the vast majority of students who are the first generation in their families to enter higher education. Since most of these students are from relatively low status backgrounds, an increase in the already significant correlation between social class and position in the tracking system of higher education is likely to occur. As more and more people enter postsecondary education, the community college will probably become more distinct from the rest of higher education both in class composition and in curriculum. With the push of the policy-planning elite for more career education, vocational training may well become more pervasive, and the community college will become even more a terminal rather than a transfer institution. These trends, often referred to as expressions of higher education's "diversity" and of the community college's "special and unique role" are the very processes which place the community college at the bottom of the class-based tracking system. The system of higher education's much-touted "diversity" is, for the most part, hierarchy rather than genuine variety (see Karabel, 1972a and 1972b), a form of hierarchy which has more to do with social class than educational philosophy.

The high rate of attrition at community colleges may well be functional for the existing social system. The cooling out function of the junior college, as Clark puts it, is what "such a college is about." Community colleges exist in part to reconcile students' culturally induced hopes for mobility with their eventual destinations, transforming structurally induced failure into individual failure. This serves to legitimize the myth of an equal opportunity structure; it shifts attention to questions of individual mobility rather than distributive justice. Cooling out, then, can be seen as conflict between working class students and standards that legitimize the position of the privileged—a veiled class conflict. Similarly, there is class conflict implicit in the differences over vocational education between the aspirations of students and the objectives of policymakers. This has occasionally become overt, but the community colleges seem to serve their legitimizing function best when the conflict remains submerged.

Can the inability of the community college movement to modify the American class structure be overcome? An assessment of some specific reforms that have been proposed may yield some insight. One obvious reform would be to reverse the pattern that Hansen and Weisbrod (1969) document—simply to invest more money in the community colleges than in the four-year public institutions. The idea of this reform would be both to provide the highest quality education to those who have socioeconomic and cognitive disadvantages to overcome and to put an end to the pattern of poor people subsidizing relatively affluent people through public systems of higher education. This proposal, which may be justified on grounds of equity, is unlikely to make much difference either in terms of education or social class. A repeated finding in social science research, confirmed by both the Coleman Report (1966) and the recent Jencks (1972) study, is that educational expenditures seem to be virtually unrelated to cognitive development at the elementary and secondary levels, and there is no reason to believe that money is any more effective in colleges. However desirable a shift in resources from four-year colleges to community colleges might be on other grounds, it is unlikely to seriously affect the larger pattern of class-based tracking in higher education.

Another possibility would be to transform the community college into a four-year institution—the very proposal that the Carnegie Commission on Higher Education strongly opposes. The purpose of this reform would be to upgrade the status of the community college and to diminish the rigidity of the tracking system. Yet it is highly questionable whether making the junior college into a senior college would have any such effect; there are marked status distinctions among four-year colleges and, in all likelihood, the new four-year institutions would be at the bottom of the prestige hierarchy. Further, the creation of more four-year colleges would probably accelerate the process of educational inflation.

The proposal to vocationalize the community college exemplifies the dilemma faced by those who would reform the public two-year college. Noting that many community college students neither transfer nor get an associate degree, proponents of vocational education argue that the students should stop engaging in a uni-dimensional academic competition which they cannot win and should instead obtain a marketable skill before leaving the educational system. If one accepts the existing system of social stratification, there is an almost irresistible logic to the vocational training argument; there are, after all, manpower shortages to be filled and it *is* true that not everyone can be a member of the elite.

In a sense, the community colleges are "damned if they do and damned if they don't." The vocational educational reform provides a striking example of their dilemma, for the question of whether community colleges should become predominantly vocational institutions may well be the most critical policy issue facing the two-year institutions in the years ahead. If they move toward more career education, they will tend to accentuate class-based tracking. If they continue as "comprehensive institutions" they will continue to be plagued by the enormous attrition in their transfer curricula. Either way, the primary role of the colleges derives from their relation to the class structure and feasible reforms will, at best, result in minor changes in their channeling function.

That the community colleges cannot do what many of their proponents claim they are supposed to do does not mean that they can do nothing at all. They do make a difference for many students— providing them opportunities for better lives than their parents had. They are able to introduce some students, particularly those who are residential rather than commuter students, to ideas, influences, and ways of life that broaden their view of the world. And surely it is not beyond reason to think that better staff, counseling, and facilities could somewhat reduce the rate of attrition in the transfer curricula. It is not beyond hope to think that reform of the vocational tracks could encourage students not to fit like cogs into rigid occupational roles but to have some faith in themselves, their right to decent working conditions, and to some control over their own work so that they could shape the roles they are supposed to fit into. It may be that students and teachers intent on changing society could raise the consciousness of community college students about where they fit in the social system and why they fit where they do. All this is possible, important, and underway in many community colleges.

But as for educational reform making this a more egalitarian society, we cannot be sanguine. Jencks (1972) has shown that the effects of schooling on ultimate income and occupation are relatively small. Even if the community colleges were to undergo a major transformation, little change in the system of social stratification would be likely to take place. If we are genuinely concerned about creating a more egalitarian society, it will be necessary to change our economic institutions. The problems of inequality and inequality of opportunity are, in short, best dealt with not through educational reform but rather by the wider changes in economic and political life that would help build a socialist society.

Writing in favor of secondary education for everybody many years ago, R. H. Tawney, the British social historian, remarked that the "intrusion into educational organization of the vulgarities of the class system is an irrelevance as mischievous in effect as it is odious in conception." That matters of social class have intruded into the community college is beyond dispute; whether the influence of class can be diminished not only in the community college but also in the larger society remains to be be seen.

REFERENCES

AGNEW, S., Toward a middle way in college admissions. *Educational Record,* 51 (Spring, 1970), pp. 106–111.

AMERICAN COUNCIL ON EDUCATION, OFFICE OF RESEARCH. National norms for entering college freshmen—Fall 1966. ACE Research Reports, Vol. 2, No. 1. Washington, D.C.: 1967.

———. The American freshman: National norms for Fall 1971. ACE Research Reports, Vol. 6, No. 6. Washington, D.C.: 1971.

BANKS, O., *Parity and prestige in English secondary education.* London: Routledge and Kegan Paul, Ltd., 1955.

BLAU, P. M., AND O. D. DUNCAN, *The American occupational structure.* New York: Wiley, 1967.

BOWLES, S., Unequal education and the reproduction of the social division of labor. *Review of radical political economics,* 3 (Fall, 1971).

BRICK, M., *Forum and focus for the junior college movement.* New York: Bureau of Publications, Teachers College, Columbia University, 1964.

BUREAU OF THE CENSUS, *The American almanac.* New York: Grosset & Dunlap, 1971a.

———, Educational attainment: March 1971. Series P20, No. 229. Washington, D.C.: U. S. Government Printing Office, 1971b.

———, Undergraduate enrollment in two-year and four-year colleges: October 1971. Series P20, No. 236. Washington, D.C.: U. S. Government Printing Office, 1972.

BUSHNELL, D. S., AND I. ZAGARIS, *Report from Project FOCUS: Strategies for change.* Washington, D.C.: American Association of Junior Colleges, 1972.

CARNEGIE COMMISSION ON HIGHER EDUCATION, *The open-door colleges.* New York: McGraw-Hill, 1970.

CLARK, B. R., *The open door college.* New York: McGraw-Hill, 1960.

———, *Educating the expert society.* San Francisco: Chandler, 1962.

COHEN, A. M. et al., *A constant variable.* San Francisco: Jossey-Bass, 1971a.

COHEN, A. M., Stretching pre-college education. *Social Policy* (May/June, 1971b), pp. 5–9.

COHEN, D. K., AND M. LAZERSON, Education and the corporate order. *Socialist Revolution,* 2 (March/April, 1972), pp. 47–72.

COLEMAN, J. S., et al., *Equality of educational opportunity.* Washington, D.C.: U. S. Government Printing Office, 1966.

COLLINS, R., Functional and conflict theories of stratification. *American Sociological Review,* 36 (December, 1971), pp. 1002–19.

COORDINATING COUNCIL FOR HIGHER EDUCATION, *The undergraduate student and his higher education: Policies of California colleges and universities in the next decade.* Sacramento, Cal., 1969.

COUNTS, G. S., *School and society in Chicago.* New York: Harcourt, Brace, 1928.

————, *The selective character of American secondary education.* Chicago: University of Chicago Press, 1922.

CROSS, K. P., The junior college student: A research description. Princeton, N.J.: Educational Testing Service, 1968.

CROSS, K. P., The role of the junior college in providing postsecondary education for all. In *Trends in postsecondary education.* Washington, D.C.: U.S. Government Printing Office, 1970.

————, *Beyond the open door.* San Francisco: Jossey-Bass, 1971.

DEPARTMENT OF HEALTH, EDUCATION, AND WELFARE. *Digest of educational statistics.* Washington, D.C.: U.S. Government Printing Office, 1970.

ETZIONI, A. The high schoolization of college. *Wall Street Journal,* March 17, 1970.

FIELDS, R. R., *The community college movement.* New York: McGraw-Hill, 1962.

FOLGER, J. K., H. S. ASTIN, AND A. E. BAYER, *Human resources and higher education.* New York: Russell Sage, 1970.

GLEAZER, E. J., JR., *This is the community college.* Boston: Houghton Mifflin, 1968.

GREER, C., *The great school legend.* New York: Basic Books, 1972.

HANSEN, W. L., AND B. A. WEISBROD, *Benefits, costs, and finance of public higher education.* Chicago: Markham, 1969.

HARRIS, N. C., The middle manpower job spectrum. In W. K. Ogilvie and M. R. Raines (Eds.), *Perspective on the community-junior college.* New York: Appleton-Century-Crofts, 1971.

HARTNETT, R. T., College and university trustees: Their backgrounds, roles, and educational attitudes. Princeton, N.J.: Educational Testing Service, 1969.

HAVEMANN, E., AND P. WEST, *They went to college.* New York: Harcourt, Brace, 1952.

HURLBURT, A. L., *State master plans for community colleges.* Washington, D.C.: American Association of Junior Colleges, 1969.

JAFFE, A. J., AND W. ADAMS, Two models of open enrollment. In L. Wilson and O. Mills (Eds.). *Universal higher education.* Washington, D.C.: American Council on Education, 1972.

JENCKS, C., AND D. RIESMAN, *The academic revolution.* Garden City, N.Y.: Doubleday, 1968.

JENCKS, C., et al., *Inequality: a reassessment of the effect of family and schooling in America.* New York: Basic Books, 1972.

KARABEL, J., Perspectives on open admissions. *Educational Record,* 53 (Winter, 1972a), pp. 30–44.

————, Open admissions: Toward meritocracy or equality? *Change,* 4 (May, 1972b), pp. 38–43.

————, AND A. W. ASTIN, Social class, academic ability, and college quality. Washington: American Council on Education, Office of Research, in press.

KARIER, C. J., Testing for order and control in the corporate liberal state. *Educational Theory*, 22 (Spring, 1972), pp. 154–180.

KATZ, M. B., *The irony of early school reform*. Boston: Beacon Press, 1968.

KENISTON, K., AND M. GERZON, Human and social benefits. In L. Wilson and O. Mills (Eds.), *Universal higher education*. Washington, D.C.: American Council on Education, 1972.

KOLKO, G., *Wealth and power in America*. New York: Praeger, 1962.

LAZERSON, M., AND W. N. GRUBB, *American education and industrialism: Documents in vocational education, 1870–1970*. New York: Teachers College, Columbia University, 1973.

LIPSET, S. M., AND R. BENDIX, *Social mobility in industrial society*. Berkeley: University of California Press, 1959.

MARLAND, S. P., JR., A strengthening alliance. In L. Wilson and O. Mills (Eds.), *Universal higher education*. Washington, D.C.: American Council on Education, 1972.

MARSHALL, T. H., *Class, citizenship, and social development*. Garden City, N.Y.: Anchor, 1965.

McDERMOTT, J., The laying on of culture. *The Nation*, March 10, 1969.

MEDSKER, L. L., AND J. W. TRENT, The influence of different types of public higher institutions on college attendance from varying socioeconomic and ability levels. Berkeley: Center for Research and Development in Higher Education, 1965.

MEDSKER, L. L., AND D. TILLERY, *Breaking the access barriers*. New York: McGraw-Hill, 1971.

MILLER, H., *Rich man, poor man*. New York: Thomas Y. Crowell, 1971.

MILNER, M., JR., *The illusion of equality*. San Francisco: Jossey-Bass, 1972.

NEWMAN, F., et al., *Report on higher education*. Reports to the U.S. Department of Health, Education, and Welfare. Washington, D.C.: U.S. Government Printing Office, 1971.

OGILVIE, W. K., Occupational education and the community college. In W. K. Ogilvie and M. R. Raines (Eds.), *Perspectives on the community-junior college*. New York: Appleton-Century-Crofts, 1971.

PIERSON, G. W., *The education of American leaders*. New York: Praeger, 1969.

POWELL, H. B., The foundation and the future of the junior college. In *The foundation and the junior college*. Washington, D.C.: American Association of Junior Colleges, 1965.

REED, R., AND H. MILLER, Some determinants of the variation in earnings for college men. *Journal of Human Resources*, 5 (Spring, 1970), pp. 177–190.

RIESSMAN, F., The 'vocationalization' of higher education: Duping the poor. *Social Policy*, 2 (May/June, 1971), pp. 3–4.

RYAN, P. B., Why industry needs the junior college. In W. K. Ogilvie and M. R. Raines (Eds.), *Perspectives on the community-junior college*. New York: Appleton-Century-Crofts, 1971.

SCHOENFELDT, L. F., Education after high school. *Sociology of Education,* 41 (Fall, 1968), pp. 350–369.

SEWELL, W. H., AND V. P. SHAH, Socioeconomic status, intelligence and the attainment of higher education. *Sociology of Education,* 40 (Winter, 1967), pp. 1–23.

SHARP, L. M., *Education and employment.* Baltimore: Johns Hopkins, 1970.

SPAETH, J. L.,The allocation of college graduates to graduate and professional schools. *Sociology of Education,* 41 (Fall, 1968), pp. 342–349.

SUNKO, THEODORE S., Making the case for junior college foundation support. In *The foundation and the junior college.* Washington, D.C.: American Association of Junior Colleges, 1965.

THORNTON, J. W., JR., *The community junior college.* New York: John Wiley, 1960.

TROW, M., The second transformation of American secondary education. In R. Bendix and S. Lipset (Eds.), *Class, status and power.* New York: Free Press, 1966.

TURNER, R., Modes of social ascent through education. In R. Bendix and S. Lipset (Eds.), *Class, status and power.* New York: Free Press, 1966.

VENN, G., *Man, education and work.* Washington, D.C.: American Council on Education, 1964.

WOLFE, A., Reform without reform: The Carnegie Commission on Higher Education. *Social Policy,* 2 (May/June, 1971), pp. 18–27.

WOLFLE, D., *The uses of talent.* Princeton, N.J.: Princeton University Press, 1971.

chapter eight

College and university trustees: Their backgrounds, roles, and educational attitudes

RODNEY T. HARTNETT

Only selected highlights from the total compilation of data are presented and interpreted here. The two most important criteria employed in deciding upon what results should be included and what emphasis they should receive were relevance and freshness: relevant to the current higher education scene, preferably to an "issue" still unresolved, and fresh, in the sense that the findings must add to what has been previously known about college and university trustees.

Thus, data regarding trustees' age, sex, level of education, income and the like are treated only briefly. On the other hand, the trustees' educational and social attitudes are dealt with in considerable detail, especially those having to do with academic freedom, business orientations, and the decision-making process. Information relating to trustees' familiarity with what has been written about higher education is discussed at some length, whereas the question of "Who shall be educated?" is, by comparison, treated very briefly, and responses to many of the questions in the survey are not discussed at all.

BIOGRAPHICAL CHARACTERISTICS

Data regarding some of the more basic characteristics of college and university trustees conform to previous findings and are not surprising in terms of the nature of the description they provide.

From Rodney T. Hartnett, *College and University Trustees: Their Backgrounds, Roles, and Educational Attitudes,* pp. 19–40. Copyright © 1969 by Educational Testing Service. All rights reserved. Reprinted by permission of the Educational Testing Service and the author.

In general, trustees are male, in their 50's (though, nationally more than a third are over 60), white (fewer than two percent in our sample are Negro), well-educated, and financially well-off (more than half have annual incomes exceeding $30,000). They occupy prestige occupations, frequently in medicine, law and education, but more often as business executives (in the total sample over 35 percent are executives of manufacturing, merchandising or investment firms and at private universities nearly 50 percent hold such positions). As a group, then, they personify "success" in the usual American sense of that word.[1]

Most are Protestants, with only four percent being Jewish and 17 percent Catholic, the majority of the latter serving on boards of Catholic institutions. Trustees also tend to identify themselves as Republicans (approximately 58 percent overall) and most often regard themselves as politically moderate (61%) rather than conservative (21%) or liberal (15%). Many of them—nearly 40 percent overall and well over half at certain types of institutions—are alumni of the institutions on whose boards they serve. Of considerable interest is the fact that for the great majority (85%) their current board membership, whether with their alma mater or not, is their only college or university trustee commitment.

EDUCATIONAL/SOCIAL ATTITUDES

Perhaps more important than biographical characteristics for understanding the college trustee is how he feels about prevailing issues that face American higher education. Indeed, the relevance of such information as occupation, income, and the like is its presumed relationship to educational attitudes. Traditionally, this relationship has been taken for granted, and some have drawn the rather reckless conclusions that because the trustee is seldom young his educational attitudes are old-fashioned, that because he is frequently a business executive he will urge that his institution be "run like a business," and so on.[2] One of our intentions in developing the questionnaire was to replace suppositions with facts, to replace easy generalities with "hard" data. To our knowledge, infor-

---

[1] Again, we caution the reader to keep in mind the purposely very general nature of these summary statements. There is considerable diversity on these characteristics across types of institutions.

[2] Of course an opposite, and perhaps more dangerous, assumption has also been frequently made: that because one is a "successful" businessman, attorney, dentist, or whatever, he will therefore be a competent overseer of a higher educational institution.

148 Rodney T. Hartnett

mation regarding trustees' opinions on most of these matters has
never before been systematically gathered on a national scale.

ACADEMIC FREEDOM

One of the prime areas of interest is that of academic freedom. A
number of items in the attitude section of the questionnaire were
directed at this issue. These items and the trustees' responses are
summarized in Table 1.

TABLE 1 EXTENT TO WHICH TRUSTEES AGREE WITH STATEMENTS RE-
GARDING ACADEMIC FREEDOM[a]

	Percentage Strongly Agreeing or Agreeing[b]	Percentage Disagreeing or Strongly Disagreeing
Faculty members have right to free expression of opinions	67	27[c]
Administration should control contents of student newspaper	40	51
Campus speakers should be screened	69	25
Students punished by local authorities for off-campus matter should also be disciplined by the college	49	38
It is reasonable to require loyalty oath from members of faculty	53	38

[a] Statements in table are abbreviated; for complete statements see questionnaire.
[b] Percentages rounded to whole numbers.
[c] Percentages do not add to 100 because of those responding "unable to say."

Though the great majority of trustees favor the right to free expression by faculty in various channels of college communication,
the more general impression one gets from these data is that the
trustees, by and large, are somewhat reluctant to accept a wider notion of academic freedom. For example, over two-thirds of these
people favor a screening process for all campus speakers, and nearly
half feel that students already punished by local authorities for involvement in matters of civil disobedience *off the campus* should be
further disciplined by the college.[3]

[3] It should be pointed out that this particular item, dealing with off-campus
civil disobedience, is probably more a matter of "in loco parentis" than academic
freedom. Nevertheless it is included here since freedom (though perhaps not
academic freedom) *is* involved, and the item does correlate with the other four in
this table.

These attitudes are extremely relevant to campus problems today. Those who would argue that the trustee holds no authority or influence need only to examine some of the trustee attitudes regarding academic freedom against a backdrop of trustee/faculty conflicts. In the fall of 1968, for example, the regents of the University of California voted to withhold regular college credits for a series of speeches by Eldridge Cleaver (Minister of Information for the Black Panthers, an Oakland-based black militant group, and author of *Soul on Ice*), at the Berkeley campus. The academic senate at Berkeley has recorded its opposition to the regents' "encroachment" in curricular matters, but, at the time of this writing, the trustees' decision stands. There are many cases similar to this one and none should come as a surprise in view of trustee attitudes.

Naturally, trustee opinions about these matters vary considerably, not only across types of institutions, as already suggested, but across other dimensions as well. As an example of this, the academic freedom attitudes reported in Table 1 are presented again in Table 2,

TABLE 2   AGREEMENT WITH ACADEMIC FREEDOM STATEMENTS BY TRUSTEES OF INSTITUTIONS IN DIFFERENT GEOGRAPHIC REGIONS (IN PERCENTAGES)[a,b]

	New England and Mid-Atlantic	South	Midwest	Rockies	West
Faculty members have right to free expression of opinions	73.2	64.0	64.2	62.6	62.0
Administration should control contents of student newspaper	29.8	51.5	42.0	48.1	44.4
Campus speakers should be screened	58.3	80.9	72.0	77.8	74.5
Students punished by local authorities for off-campus matter should also be disciplined by the college	39.8	63.2	49.5	62.5	44.0
It is reasonable to require loyalty oaths from faculty members	46.4	63.6	52.2	66.1	53.4

[a] Numbers are percentages agreeing or strongly agreeing with each statement.
[b] Statements in table are abbreviated; for complete statements see questionnaire.

this time arranged by geographic region. The diversity is apparent. Notice, for example, that over half of the trustees of institutions located in the South agree that the contents of the student newspaper should be controlled by the institution, whereas only about 30 percent of the trustees of New England and Mid-Atlantic institutions hold similar views. Similar comparisons suggest that, in general, trustees of southern and Rocky Mountain institutions are most cautious in these matters, whereas trustees of institutions located in the New England and Mid-Atlantic region appear to be the most "liberal." The point of this particular analysis is to underscore the fact that the total sample of trustees could be categorized many different ways—by type of control, geographic region, enrollment, and sex makeup of student body to name but a few—and differences would almost surely appear.

There is an interesting sidelight to the academic freedom data which is not presented in Tables 1 or 2, but can be seen by referring to attitude items 3, 4, 5, 16 and 20 in Part II of [the original] report. Trustees of public junior colleges appear to be the least freedom-oriented in terms of their responses to these items. At the same time we note that 42 percent of the trustees of public junior colleges are elected by the general public (item 5 in questionnaire Part III [of the original report]). Though such an occurrence is far too tenuous to draw any definite conclusions some speculations are hard to resist. In a recent discussion of the matter, Jencks and Riesman remark, "Publicly elected or appointed boards of trustees seem in many ways to cause more trouble than they are worth." [4] This opinion apparently stems from their belief that "budgetary support and review are the only forms of public control that make much sense" and that these functions could just as easily, and more efficiently, be performed by already existing groups (for example, the legislature). As suggested by comments of these same authors in another source, however, we may wonder if their opinion isn't also influenced by the numerous cases in which trustees have campaigned for a position on an institution's governing board on a plank opposed to academic freedom. [5] The public often does not understand the full meaning of academic freedom and is apparently suspicious of it. It is possible, therefore, that publicly elected trustees may be conservative in these matters, as suggested by the junior college data reported here. [6]

If this is true, it would suggest that publicly elected trustees may not be confronted with the long-standing dilemma facing other governing board members, that is, whether to adopt the role of

[4] Jencks, Christopher, and Riesman, David. *The Academic Revolution.* New York: Doubleday, 1968, p. 269.

[5] Riesman, David, and Jencks, Christopher. "The Viability of the American College," in *The American College* (Nevitt Sanford, editor). New York: Wiley, 1962, p. 109.

[6] The general question of what differences exist, if any, among trustees gaining board membership by different avenues is one of many we hope to pursue in much greater detail in subsequent analyses of these data.

"protector of the public interest" or that of insulator between the public and the institution. While most trustees—at least at public institutions—appear to vacillate between these two roles, the publicly elected trustee, perhaps by virtue of being elected rather than appointed, is apparently committed to the former.[7]

EDUCATION FOR WHOM?

Another topic of recent concern to American higher education has to do with the question of "education for whom?" Until fairly recently American higher education was restricted to those of demonstrated academic ability who could afford the high costs that earning a degree required. More recently, however, we have seen a trend toward more flexible selection criteria and an "open-door" philosophy, perhaps exemplified best by the growing number of junior colleges throughout the country. Trustee attitudes toward this phenomenon are summarized in Table 3.

TABLE 3   TRUSTEES' VIEWS REGARDING WHO SHOULD BE SERVED BY HIGHER EDUCATION[a]

	Percentage Strongly Agreeing or Agreeing[b]	Percentage Disagreeing or Strongly Disagreeing
Attendance a privilege, not a right	92	6[c]
Aptitude most important admissions criteria	70	24
Curriculum designed to accommodate diverse student body	63	27
Opportunity for higher education for anyone who desires it	85	11
College should admit socially disadvantaged who do not meet normal requirements	66	22

[a] Statements in table are abbreviated; for complete statements see questionnaire.
[b] Percentages rounded to whole numbers.
[c] Percentages do not add to 100 because of those responding "unable to say."

For the national sample taken together, there appears to be general sympathy for the broader-access trend just discussed. Slightly more than 85 percent agree (with almost one-third *strongly* agreeing) that there should be opportunities for higher education avail-

[7] For a more detailed discussion of these roles at both public and private institutions, see John D. Millett, *The Academic Community: An Essay on Organization.* New York: McGraw-Hill, Inc., 1962.

able to anyone who seeks education beyond secondary school, and two-thirds agree that colleges should admit socially disadvantaged students who appear to have the potential, even when these students do not meet the normal entrance requirements. Nevertheless over 90 percent still regard attendance at their college to be a privilege, not a right. In fact, 68 percent of the trustees of public junior colleges, open-door institutions if you will, also share the privilege-not-a-right sentiment. In view of the other responses indicating acceptance of the concept of wide accessibility of higher education opportunity, these latter figures seem inconsistent. Several explanations seem plausible, however. It may mean that even trustees of non-selective institutions cling to the elitist model, perhaps thinking that while *other* colleges should employ flexible admissions criteria, their own institution must "maintain high standards." Or perhaps most trustees simply interpreted the statement somewhat differently, wishing only to indicate their feeling that students should not *expect* to be in college but, rather, should feel *grateful* for the opportunity. Or finally, it could mean that trustees favor extending the opportunity for college *admission* to more and more students but, in order to protect themselves and their institutions against "unacceptable" student conduct, feel the institutions must retain the authority to decide who will *remain.*

BUSINESS ORIENTATION OF TRUSTEES

One frequently hears the assertion that trustees tend to think colleges and universities can function best by imitating the corporation or big business model (the assumption being that such a model is inappropriate and, in the long run, damaging to higher education). Whether such a model is appropriate or not cannot be answered by these data, but we can at least get some idea of whether or not it is a model preferred by the trustees.

It has already been indicated that trustees are frequently business executives. Two additional indices should also suggest such an orientation: first, whether trustees endorse the statement that "running a college is basically like running a business," and, second, the extent to which they feel "experience in high-level business management" is an important quality to consider in the selection of a new president. These data are presented in Table 4.

Inspection of this table makes it clear that trustees who are business executives definitely have a stronger business orientation toward the university than trustees with other occupations. For the total sample, of the 35 percent who are business executives nearly

TABLE 4   TRUSTEE RESPONSES TO ITEMS INDICATIVE OF THEIR BUSINESS-MODEL ORIENTATION FOR COLLEGES AND UNIVERSITIES (IN PERCENTAGES)

	Regard Themselves as Executives of Manufacturing, Merchandising or Banking Firm	Agree That Running a College is Basically Like Running a Business		Regard Experience in High-level Business Management as Important Quality for New President	
	(col. 1)	(col. 2) Business Executives[a]	(col. 3) Others	(col. 4) Business Executives	(col. 5) Others
TOTAL SAMPLE	35	49	31	49	44
Public junior colleges	33 (7)[b]	56 (2)	49	45 (6)	46
Public colleges	39 (3)	56 (2)	42	55 (1)	40
Public universities	36 (5)	45 (6)	28	51 (4)	43
Private colleges	36 (5)	48 (4)	29	49 (5)	45
Private universities	49 (1)	42 (7)	23	41 (7)	38
Catholic colleges and universities	22 (8)	56 (2)	31	54 (2)	43
Selective public	36 (5)	47 (5)	30	53 (3)	38
Selective private	43 (2)	30 (8)	14	31 (8)	25

[a] "Business executives" includes all those in first column, determined on the basis of their response to the occupation item (#16) in first part of questionnaire.

[b] Numbers in parentheses alongside percentages in columns 1, 2, and 4 are within-column ranks (excluding total sample). Rank-order correlations (ρ) between columns are as follows: $\rho_{12} = -.62$ (p $<$ .05), $\rho_{14} = -.40$ (n.s.), $\rho_{24} = +.69$ (p $<$ .05).

half (49%) agree that running a college is basically like running a business, whereas fewer than one-third (31%) of the nonexecutives accept this view. In fact, of the 16 possible business executives vs. "other" comparisons (eight institutional types by two attitude items) there is only one case in which trustees who are business executives are not also more business oriented. The exception is for public junior colleges, where a slightly higher proportion of nonbusiness executives regard business management experience as an important quality for a new president. Thus, there appears to be validity to the often heard claim that because governing boards are made up of businessmen, the decisions they make about the institutions will reflect this business outlook.

Another finding emerging from the data in Table 4, however, has to do with the relationship between the three indices and suggests that the "business outlook" hypothesis is not so simple. Note that the group having the second greatest proportion of trustees who are

business executives (selective private universities) is the group which
has the smallest percentage of those executives agreeing that running a college is like running a business and also the smallest proportion regarding high-level business management experience as an
important criterion for a new president. Contrast this with trustees
of public junior colleges, where a nearly opposite pattern occurs. In
fact, the rank-order correlations between columns indicates that,
across all types, the proportion of trustees holding business-executive
positions is *negatively* correlated with the proportion of those executives endorsing the attitude statements in Table 4; that is, the greater
the proportion of business executives on the governing board, the
smaller the proportion of executives who feel that "running a college is like running a business" and that high-level business management experience is an important quality to consider in choosing a
new president. Consequently, even though the "business orientation"
is distinctly more prevalent among business executives generally, it
would be a mistake to jump to the conclusion that on boards where
the proportion of business executives is high, the business orientation will be strongest.

What is the explanation for this befuddling situation? One is at
first tempted to speculate about the influence of the nonbusiness
trustees on their colleagues' attitudes. While such a possibility
should not be lightly dismissed, a more convincing interpretation
might consider the varying levels of "executiveness" represented on
the boards. We suspect, for example, that the types of institutions
having the greatest proportion of business executives (the private
universities and selective private institutions) generally have men
who are a much different kind of executive than those who serve on
boards with the smallest proportion of businessmen (the junior colleges and Catholic institutions). This is probably a case of men
simply not being cut from the same cloth, regardless of what may be
suggested by the mutual occupational perception of "business executive." This difference, in turn, is reflected in their attitudes about
"running" a college, and the high-level executive appears to be more
inclined to see it as a nonbusiness undertaking when compared to
his probably less prestigious executive counterpart serving on some
of the other boards.

THE DECISION-MAKING PROCESS

One of the complaints most frequently made about higher education by disenchanted members of the academic community is that
the wrong people are making the decisions. Many of the campus

demonstrators have been claiming, in one way or another, that the university should be run by the faculty and students, not by administrators and trustees. The following quotation, taken from a newspaper article summarizing some of the events at Columbia in the spring of 1968, is not atypical:

> Speakers in buildings and on the lawn . . . called for the "reconstruction of this university," with students and faculty assuming the power now exercised by the president and trustees.[8]

Though the extent to which faculty and students across the country actually feel they should "run" the campus is not known, there are some indications that it is not just a radical minority who desire more participation in the decision-making process. In a survey of faculty opinion regarding participation in academic decision making at one institution, for example, 51 percent of the faculty included in the survey felt that "the faculty has too little influence on decisions; more of the decision making power should rest with the faculty," and another 44 percent agreed that "the faculty's role is not what it should be ideally, but it is about what one can realistically expect." Furthermore, 63 percent indicated that they were either dissatisfied or very dissatisfied with this situation.[9] And a recent survey of college trustees, administrators, faculty members, and students conducted by the American Council on Education, tells us that faculty are almost unanimous in wanting a larger share in academic rule, including greater participation in the selection of their president.[10] Though the former study was done at one university in the Midwest, and the faculty sample in the A.C.E. study consisted only of American Association of University Professors chapter heads (thus making neither sample "representative" in any sense), together they provide some empirical support for the claim that there is dissatisfaction with the perceived way in which decisions are reached.

With this information in mind, let us examine the trustees' views of who should have major involvement in deciding various campus issues. Several things are made quite clear by these data, which are presented in Tables 5 and 6.

[8] Kramer, Joel. "Does Student Power Mean: Rocking the Boat? Running the University?" *New York Times.* May 26, 1968, section IV, p. 32.

[9] Dykes, Archie R. *Faculty Participation in Academic Decision Making.* American Council on Education, 1968.

[10] Caffrey, John. "Predictions for Higher Education in the 1970's," in *The Future Academic Community: Continuity and Change,* background papers for participants in the 51st annual meeting of the American Council on Education, 1968, pp. 123–153.

TABLE 5 PROPORTION OF TRUSTEES WHO THINK THAT CERTAIN CAM-
PUS GROUPS SHOULD HAVE MAJOR AUTHORITY IN MAKING VARIOUS
DECISIONS (IN PERCENTAGES)[a,b]

	Decision should be made by administrators alone (A), trustees alone (T) or trustees and admin. together (TA)				Decision should be made by faculty alone or in conjunction with admin., trustees or both	Decision should be made by students alone or in conjunction with faculty and/or A and/or T
				(col. 1)	(col. 2)	(col. 3)
	A	T	TA	Total[c]		
Add or delete courses	11	1	4	16	65	14
Add or delete degree programs	9	6	18	33	57	3
Rules re student housing	32	2	13	47	6	37
Commencement speaker	29	4	13	46	25	22
Presidential appointment	1	64	5	70	8	1
Determine tuition	10	17	64	91	2	1
Professor's immoral conduct	29	7	28	64	27	2
Tenure decisions	27	7	30	64	30	1
Student cheating	20	0	1	21	39	37
Policy re student protests	16	6	30	52	18	22
Appoint academic dean	22	8	33	63	30	1
Policy re faculty leaves	19	8	31	58	37	0
Admission criteria	17	3	16	36	59	1
Honorary degrees	7	19	31	57	34	1
Athletic program	17	4	22	43	22	24
Fraternities and sororities	18	5	21	44	10	31

[a] Statements in table are abbreviated; for complete statements see questionnaire
[b] Percentages rounded to whole numbers.
[c] Column 1, which is simply a total of columns A, T, and TA, can be interpreted as the
percentage of trustees who feel that faculty and/or students should *not* have major
authority in deciding the various issues.

First, trustees generally favor a hierarchical system in which decisions are made at the top and passed "down." For example, over 50
percent of the total sample of trustees believe that faculty and students should *not* have major authority in half of the sixteen decisions listed (that is, eight column-one percentage figures exceed 50
percent in Table 5). The proportion feeling that trustees and/or

administrators alone should have major authority in making the decision exceeds 40 percent in 12 of the 16 decisions.[11] Some of these are particularly interesting. For example, 63 percent say that the appointment of an academic dean should be made with only the administrators and trustees having major authority, or, to say it another way, 63 percent feel that the faculty should *not* have major authority in the appointment of their dean. Similarly 57 percent would exempt the faculty from major authority in the awarding of honorary degrees, and 58 percent would exempt them from major authority in policies regarding faculty leaves. To many, of course, these findings come as no surprise. But, surprising or not, they do help underscore some of the very wide differences of opinion among members of the academic community as to who should govern.

Second, there is a perceptible difference in the kinds of decisions trustees feel should and should not involve other groups having substantial authority. For example, the areas that should have greatest faculty authority are seen to be, by and large, academic matters, such as whether or not to add or delete specific courses, or what criteria should be employed in admitting students. Student authority is judged relevant in matters of student life, such as housing, student cheating, fraternities and sororities, and the like.

Third, though the trustees generally prefer an arrangement in which the faculty and students do not have major authority, neither do they want to "rule" by themselves. Notice in Table 5, for example, that with the exception of presidential appointments, they prefer major authority for decisions to rest with the administration alone or with the administration and trustees conjointly. Thus, the "power at the top" model must be modified. Trustees prefer their own power to be singularly authoritative only when it comes to choosing the president of the institution. Having selected him, however, they like to lean heavily on him (and his administrative colleagues) for making the decisions.[12]

Finally, as seen in Table 6, there is a great deal of variation from

[11] Caution should be used in interpreting Table 5. It should be kept in mind, for example, that the percentages in columns two and three might also include trustees and administrators, and column three might also include faculty members. Column one, then, is the only "pure" combination. Again, the reader is urged to study Part II of [the original] report.

[12] It should be remembered that these data refer to how trustees think decisions *should* be made, not how they *are* made. They are trustee preferences. As suggested in the introduction to this report, many claim that the trustees' real authority has diminished substantially over the years to a point where the gap between "paper" power and actual power is large indeed. For a more complete discussion of this, see Ernest L. Boyer, "A Fresh Look at the College Trustee," *Educational Record*, Summer, 1968, pp. 274–279.

TABLE 6 PERCENTAGE OF TRUSTEES BY TYPE OF INSTITUTION FEELING THAT VARIOUS DECISIONS SHOULD BE MADE WITH ADMINISTRATORS AND/OR TRUSTEES HAVING THE ONLY MAJOR AUTHORITY

Decision	TOTAL	Public J.C.	Public Colleges	Public Univ.	Private Colleges	Private Univ.	Catholic C's & U's	Selective Public	Selective Private
Add or delete courses	16	31	21	17	14	10	13	13	6
Add or delete degree programs	33	56	42	32	31	25	31	26	18
Rules re student housing	47	54	55	53	46	47	37	48	40
Commencement speaker	46	52	49	46	46	48	44	39	44
Presidential appointment	70	85	72	60	69	70	70	61	63
Determine tuition	91	91	87	88	93	93	88	88	95
Professor's immoral conduct	64	74	70	67	65	60	56	63	54
Tenure decisions	64	79	67	61	67	55	54	63	44
Student cheating	21	26	27	24	19	20	20	14	19
Policy re student protests	52	64	60	61	51	54	45	63	49
Appoint academic dean	63	81	68	57	64	61	61	48	54
Policy re faculty leaves	58	70	65	60	59	54	46	57	48
Admissions criteria	36	56	50	41	33	27	33	47	25
Honorary degrees	57	64	62	48	55	51	60	43	45
Athletic programs	43	49	58	50	41	42	41	48	37
Fraternities and sororities	44	95	48	47	45	47	38	43	44
No. of issues with 50% or more trustees feeling trustees and/or administrators alone should have major authority	8	13	11	9	8	8	6	6	4

group to group on these matters. It would appear that trustees of selective private institutions are most inclined to include other members of the academic community in the decision-making process, while trustees of non-selective public institutions are more inclined toward a power-at-the-top sort of arrangement. Notice, for example, that 50 percent or more of the trustees feel that administrators and/or trustees alone should have major authority in deciding 13 of the 16 issues at public junior colleges, but only 4 of the 16 issues at selective private institutions. The concept of democratic governance or shared authority clearly has a more receptive audience among trustees at the latter type of institution. In fact, the ordering of institutions in Table 6 would correspond very closely to an ordering of institutional types by educational prestige. That is, where prestige is defined by the usual (but not necessarily reasonable) indices of student ability, faculty prominence and the like, it would appear that the greater the prestige of the institutional type, the more likely the trustees are to favor student and faculty involvement in decision making.[13] It can also be seen that, with the exception of the selective public universities, there is public-private division on this question.

It would be easy to get caught in a chicken vs. egg cycle in trying to account for these relationships, and there surely is no simple explanation. But again, speculation is hard to resist, and several interpretations are compelling. The most basic reason for the public-private difference probably comes from the sources of financial support. Because they do not have to answer to a public constituency, trustees of private institutions may be more willing to maintain a looser hold on the reins. Though accountable to the alumni, parents, and "friends" of the institution, such groups are basically *for* the institution and are seldom as concerned about its actions as the general public might be of colleges supported by tax money. Thus, trustees of private institutions are less hesitant to involve the faculty and students.

The reason for the prestige difference is not as straightforward but certainly no less important. There is a relationship between institutional prestige and trustee affluence. More specifically, the greater the prestige of the institution, the higher the trustees' in-

[13] There is corroborating data for this assertion. In other research currently underway in the Higher Education Research Group at ETS, scores on the Democratic Governance scale of an experimental *Institutional Functioning Inventory* (an instrument which asks for faculty perceptions of their own institutions) have been found to correlate significantly with selectivity, income per student, proportion of faculty holding a doctorate, and average faculty compensation.

come, level of education, occupational status, etc.[14] Such people
are probably more inclined to delegate authority and to be less concerned personally about maintaining control over things. Trustees
of the more prestigious institutions, by virtue of the characteristics
that led to their being selected to such boards, are simply more inclined to a laissez faire attitude regarding student and faculty involvement in campus governance.

In any event, the question "who shall govern" is obviously a very
complex one and to be treated thoroughly would require far more
detailed treatment than provided by the brief summary of responses
reported here. Many faculty who complain about lack of participation in academic governance are actually unwilling to participate
themselves and suspicious of other members of the faculty who do
get involved. Furthermore, it is sometimes members of the faculty
who would prefer to keep authority out of the hands of their colleagues. As one recent example of this, at an institution which is
moving from a teachers' college to a large state university, one department chairman opposed efforts to give greater authority to faculty members on the grounds that there were still far too many
holdovers on the faculty from the teacher-training days who were
not at all interested in research and presumably would have slowed
the institution's emergence as a first-rate institution.[15]

Nevertheless, it seems safe to conclude that, by and large, faculty
members tend to favor a horizontal as opposed to vertical form of
authority, whereas trustees prefer a hierarchical arrangement or
system of graded authority, imitating, it would seem, the "bureaucratic management" model. Though neither of these forms of government actually exist in any pure sense, they still represent what
would appear to be rather basic ideological differences between
trustees and faculty.

POLITICAL PREFERENCE AND IDEOLOGY

A summary of the trustees' political party affiliation, political ideology, and the relationship between these two variables is presented

[14] See data in Part II [of the original report].
[15] Rourke, Francis and Brooks, Glenn. *The Managerial Revolution in Higher
Education.* Baltimore: The Johns Hopkins Press, 1966, p. 117. Readers interested
in more detailed discussions of this problem should see *Faculty Participation in
Academic Governance,* a report of the AAHE Task Force on Faculty Representation and Academic Negotiations, Campus Governance Program (1967), and a report of a study by Archie R. Dykes, *op. cit.*

TABLE 7   CLASSIFICATION OF TRUSTEES BY POLITICAL PARTY PREFER-
ENCE AND IDEOLOGY (IN PERCENTAGES)

	Conservative	Moderate	Liberal	Total[a]
Republican	16.95	39.53	4.06	60.54
Democrat	3.74	20.32	10.50	34.56
Other	0.91	2.69	1.31	4.91
TOTAL	21.60	62.54	15.87	100%

Note: The correlation (contingency coefficient) between party affiliation and political ideology is .32 (p < .01), i.e., there is a tendency for those who are Republicans
to also be conservative, etc.

[a] The data in this table include only those trustees who indicated both their party
preference and ideology. Therefore it differs slightly from the data reported on page
20 and in Part II [of the original report].

in Table 7. Of the trustees who indicated both their party preference and ideology, over 60 percent described themselves as Republican and slightly less than 35 percent as Democrat. The majority
regard themselves as moderates, 21.6 percent as conservatives, and
15.9 percent as liberals. Furthermore, there was an interaction or
correlation between these characteristics. We note the tendency for
Republicans to regard themselves more often as conservative than
liberal (approximately 17% vs. 4%) and for Democrats to view
themselves more often as liberals than conservatives (10.5% vs.
3.7%).

Contrast this profile of the trustee with that of the college faculty
member. In general, one gets a much different picture, with most
reports indicating that the majority of college faculty members are
Democrats.[16] Furthermore, though we can cite no research evidence
for this claim, it is extremely unlikely that 22 percent of the faculty
would regard themselves as conservatives (though we do suspect
that conservative trustees tend to be at the same institutions as con-

[16] However, there is variation across academic fields. Charles G. McClintock,
Charles B. Spaulding, and Henry A. Turner, who have reported on the political
orientations of academic psychologists (*American Psychologist*, 20, 1965), political
scientists (*Western Political Quarterly*, 16, 1963), and sociologists (*Sociology and
Social Research*, 47, 1963), report that over two thirds of the social scientists regard themselves as Democrats. But a recent multidiscipline study (Charles B.
Spaulding and Henry A. Turner, *Sociology of Education*, Summer, 1968) indicates
that political preference differences are associated with different orientations of
the disciplines toward social criticism or toward the applications of knowledge in
business and industry. Thus, they found engineers and mathematicians, for example, to lean toward the Republican Party. See also an older source, Paul F.
Lazarsfeld and Wagner Thielens, *The Academic Mind*, Glencoe, Illinois: The
Free Press, 1958.

servative faculty). With such a gap in the political orientations of these two groups, then, it should hardly come as a surprise to find disagreement over educational matters, for both party affiliation and political ideology are related to the attitude items already discussed.[17] On the basis of correlational data, for example, we note a definite tendency for trustees who regard themselves as conservatives to endorse such statements (see Table 1) as "the administration should exercise control over the contents of the student newspaper" $(r = .37)$, and "the requirement that a professor sign a loyalty oath is reasonable" $(r = .47)$.

Most academicians would probably attach a negative value to such facts, but it should be pointed out that, as with most situations of this kind, there are two sides to the coin. Jencks and Riesman, for example, offer cogent arguments that, at least until quite recently, it has been the Republican moderates, not the Democrats, who have led the struggle for more generous university appropriations.[18] These are obviously not simple matters.

The party preference data in Table 7 are also reflected in the extent to which the trustees feel that their political or social views are similar to various well-known (usually political) figures. Of the 18 persons listed in the questionnaire, only two received similarity-of-view endorsements from more than 60 percent of the total trustee sample. These were Richard Nixon (62%), and Nelson Rockefeller (68%). . . .

---

[17] The trustees' disagreement is not just with faculty members. As reported in Caffrey's study (*op. cit.*), when college students, faculty, administrators and trustees were asked to indicate the desirability of various events occurring (in higher education) in the next ten years, faculty and students were in greater agreement with each other than either was with trustees (p. 135).

[18] Jencks and Riesman, *op cit.*, pp. 277–279.

c h a p t e r   n i n e

Higher education
and capitalist society

RALPH MILIBAND

There is no dispute about the fact—it is indeed the merest commonplace—that with the exception of some private institutions of higher learning, notably in the United States, the universities are very largely dependent upon the state for finance in the pursuit of their main activities, namely teaching and research. One obvious consequence of that fact is that the state has come to have an increasing say, directly or indirectly, in the manner in which the universities use the funds which are allotted to them. For the United States, Professor Clark Kerr has noted that, in 1960, "higher education received about 1.5 billion [dollars] from the federal government—a hundredfold increase in twenty years";[1] and he further observes that "clearly, the shape and nature of university research are profoundly affected by federal monies." [2] Indeed, in his valedictory "military-industrial complex" speech, President Eisenhower went as far as to suggest that "the free university, historically the fountainhead of free ideas and scientific discovery, has experienced a revolution in the conduct of research. Partly because of the huge cost involved, a government contract becomes virtually a substitute for intellectual curiosity." [3] This is probably somewhat overdrawn; more apposite is the notion that a government contract, and subsidies generally, tend to *direct* intellectual

"Higher Education and Capitalist Society" (editors' title). From Ralph Miliband, *The State in Capitalist Society* (New York: Basic Books, Inc., 1969), pp. 246–59, 260–61. © 1969 by George Weidenfeld & Nicolson, Ltd., Publishers, London, Basic Books, Inc., Publishers, New York. Reprinted by permission of George Weidenfeld & Nicolson, Ltd., Basic Books, Inc., and the author.

[1] Clark Kerr, *The Uses of the University*, 1963, p. 53.
[2] *Ibid.*, p. 53.
[3] Quoted in Cook, *The Warfare State*, 1963, p. 3.

curiosity in certain fields rather than in others, notably that of
"defence." The point also applies in full measure to universities
in other countries; the state everywhere now plays an important,
even a decisive part in determining how, both in teaching and research, universities may play their part in "serving the community."
Thus, quite apart from the government itself, the University Grants
Committee in Britain has come to assume a much more positive
role than in the past and now views it as its task "to assist, in con-
sultation with the universities and other bodies concerned, the
preparation and execution of such plans for the development of
the universities as may from time to time be required to ensure
that they are fully adequate to national needs." [4] The degree of
control, intervention and direction which this implies may con-
fidently be expected to grow.

But while such a development is inevitable, and may in certain
limited respects be even deemed desirable, it has also in the particular context in which it occurs certain important implications which
advocates of state intervention tend to ignore.[5] Professor Clark Kerr
also suggests that "the university has become a prime instrument
of national purpose";[6] and this is echoed by a former Rector of the
University of Orléans, who speaks of the university as the "collec-
tivité responsable de la mission la plus essentielle à l'avenir national
—avec la Défense *et faisant d'ailleurs de plus en plus partie de
celle-ci.*" [7] But the "national purpose" or the "mission" of which
the universities become an instrument, "prime" or otherwise, is
something to the determination of which they themselves, as universities, naturally make no contribution. In other words, what they
serve is, using the word literally, an alien purpose, that of the state.
And not only do they serve it; by so doing, they identify themselves
with it, and accept it as legitimate, worthy of support.

Universities and their spokesmen very often seek to eschew such
an explicit commitment. Lord Robbins, in an address delivered to
the assembly of European rectors and vice-chancellors at Göttingen
in 1964 may well have been expressing a common sentiment when
he said that the duty of universities was to advance

[4] W. Mansfield Cooper, "Change in Britain," in W. Mansfield Cooper *et al.,
Governments and the University,* 1966, p. 7.
[5] See, e.g., R. O. Berdahl, "University-State Relations Re-examined," in P.
Halmos (ed.), *Sociological Studies in British University Education,* 1963.
[6] Kerr, *The Uses of the University,* p. 87.
[7] G. Antoine and J. C. Passeron, *La Réforme de l'Université,* 1966, p. 25 (my
italics).

. . . the habit of social judgement in terms of consequences rather than categories. We must assess the value of actions, not in terms of pre-established classification according to this or that *a priori* ethic, but rather in terms of their effect on human happiness. We must teach that the maxim, *let justice be done if the skies fall,* comes from the childhood of the race; and that, on any civilised assessment, the falling of the skies is one of the consequences which have to be taken into account before we can say whether a certain course of action is, or is not, just.[8]

But the "civilised assessment" of which Lord Robbins speaks is much more likely to be interpreted in conservative ways than in dissenting ones. On the whole, the university, as an institution, has seldom refused to serve the "national purpose," as defined by the state, and has found it relatively easy to rationalise its accept-ance in terms of its own proclaimed ideals. From this point of view, the notion that universities, as distinct from some of those who work in them, are centres of dissent is a piece of mythology. If anything, the university, including the majority of its teachers, has always tended, particularly in times of great national crisis, and precisely when acute moral issues were involved, to take a poor view of its dissenters, staff and students, and quite often to help the state by acting against them. As Professor MacIver has noted, "there is no evidence to confirm the charge that educators are markedly radical. On the contrary, such evidence as we have sug-gests that they tend on the whole to the conservative side." [9] This is not to underestimate the minority, sometimes the sizeable minor-ity, which has, as in the United States in regard to the war in Vietnam, refused to identify itself with the "national purpose" as defined by the state. In fact, that minority everywhere is now prob-ably larger, proportionately, than at any time in the past. As higher education expands to meet the needs of the economic system, so does it also come to include more and more teachers who do con-ceive their vocation as requiring them to insist that "let justice be done if the skies fall," and who do therefore find themselves at odds with an unjust society and with a state which expresses its in-justices. Nevertheless, it is still the case that the great majority of academics in these countries have found little or no difficulty in reconciling their vocation with support for the "national purpose,"

[8] Lord Robbins, *The University in the Modern World,* 1966, p. 15 (italics in text).
[9] R. MacIver, *Academic Freedom in Our Time,* 1955, p. 132.

whatever that purpose may have been.[10] Indeed, many American academics have been not only willing but eager to place their skills at the service of *any* policy their government has chosen to pursue. As Professor Riesman has noted, "American scholars, despite our country's tradition of pluralism and foreign study, are for the most part readily enlisted in an era of total war and total loyalty." [11] But it bears repeating that academics elsewhere are no different, in this respect, from their American counterparts—American academics have only, in recent years, had greater opportunities.

This points to another large change which has come over university life. Not only is the state more involved in the university; academics are also immeasurably more involved than ever before in the life of the state. Lord Bowden has said of the United States that

... dons are everywhere in Washington—they run the science policy committees, they advise the president himself and most of his department heads. . . . The universities themselves are an essential component of this new machine. The system depends on free and frequent interchange of staff between the government, business and the academic world.[12]

Quoting this, Professor McConnell has a comment which seems singularly apposite:

In this interchange [he writes] . . . the universities have almost certainly lost some of their prerogative to criticise, some of their freedom to speak out on controversial political and economic issues. President Clark Kerr of the University of California, as did President Eisenhower when he left office, warned that the alliance between industry and the Department of Defence might exert excessive influence on national policy. President Kerr might also have warned of the possible dangers to the integrity of the university from the military-industrial-university complex.[13]

This is not, it should be clear, simply a matter of academics producing material which may be of use in the determination of public policy, but of the assumption by academics of an official

[10] For a useful discussion of the moral and political postures of American social scientists in recent years, see T. Roszak (ed.), *The Dissenting Academy*, 1967; C. W. Mills, *The Sociological Imagination*, 1959; and P. Lazarsfeld and W. Thielens Jr., *The Academic Mind. Social Scientists in a Time of Crisis*, 1958.

[11] D. Riesman, *Constraint and Variety in American Education*, 1956, p. 90.

[12] T. R. McConnell, "Governments and University—A Comparative Analysis," in Mansfield Cooper *et al.*, *Governments and the University*, pp. 89–90.

[13] *Op. cit.*, p. 90.

role, of their entry into government service on a part-time or, temporarily, on a full-time basis. There may well be academics whose independence of mind and whose critical powers—assuming they were there in the first place—are not eroded by this involvement with the world of office and power. But it is at least as likely that, for most academics, that involvement produces an "understanding" of the "problems" of government which makes for a kind of "responsible" criticism that bears a remarkable resemblance to more or less sophisticated apologetics. Such men are often senior and eminent academics; their contribution to the "officialisation" of university thought and behaviour ought not to be underestimated.

Apart from the state, the most important influence on universities is that of the business world. This is so for many reasons. For one thing, more and more academics are now drawn into that world as consultants and advisers; and just as those academics who are involved with the state may be expected to import into their universities a "responsible" appreciation of the official point of view, so may those who have close contact with the world of business be expected to exhibit, in their work as academics, a lively appreciation of the virtues and purposes of private enterprise. Like their "officialised" colleagues in relation to government, they too are most likely to show an acute "understanding" of the "problems" of business. As Professor McConnell puts it in regard to both:

Some of the dangers of allying the university with government and industry are obvious. Others are subtle. I believe a careful study would show that, increasingly, the values of the academic man have become the values of the market place or the governmental arena and not the values of the free intellect. The age of faculty and university affluence has exalted economic advantage at the expense of human and humane values.[14]

Secondly, private institutions of higher learning, notably in the United States, are largely dependent for financial support on wealthy individuals, either businessmen or others, and on corporate enterprise. But even universities which rely mainly on financial support from the state find benefactions, gifts and endowments very useful, and these similarly come mainly from the world of business and from members of the dominant classes. The largesse which private benefactors have displayed towards universities has often been celebrated as a tangible proof of the sense of social re-

[14] *Op. cit.*, pp. 90-1.

sponsibility and "soulfulness" of corporations, and of wealthy men generally. But however this may be, the impact of such benefactions, and the knowledge that they are to be had, is not likely to produce among the actual or potential recipients an attitude of critical independence towards the benefactors or towards the activities which make the benefactions possible in the first place. Thus a Business School largely endowed by business, and whose teachers enjoy a close and cordial relation to the world of business, cannot be expected to find much that is radically wrong with private enterprise—even though the endowment is altogether without strings. Similarly a university research project sponsored and financed by business is most likely to be conducted within the framework of assumptions and values of the "business community"; and its results are equally unlikely to be of a kind acutely displeasing to the sponsors.

Thirdly, businessmen and other "leaders of the community," whose ideological dispositions are not likely to run to radicalism, dominate the boards of trustees, regents or governors in whom the ultimate control of universities is vested; and while the point has been most often made in regard to the United States, it applies with equal force to other systems where lay governors play a role in institutions of higher learning. For the United States, Professor MacIver has noted that "in the non-governmental institutions, the typical board member is associated with large-scale business, a banker, manufacturer, business executive, or prominent lawyer. His income falls in a high bracket." [15] An older study, published in 1947, noted also that the 734 trustees of thirty leading universities were "divided about equally between the professions on the one hand, and proprietors, managers and officials on the other." Of the latter group, "bankers, brokers and financiers" and "manufacturing entrepreneurs and executives" were by far the largest group; and for the professional group, lawyers and judges were the largest element, followed by clergymen.[16] As far as known party preferences are concerned, 61 percent were Republicans and 35 percent Democrats, the likelihood being that the percentage of Republicans was higher for the total group.[17] This study was based upon the years 1934–5. But, as Professor Domhoff has recently argued,[18] "there is no reason to believe that the dominance of the

[15] MacIver, *Academic Freedom in Our Time*, p. 78.
[16] H. P. Beck, *Men Who Control Our Universities*, 1947, pp. 51 ff.
[17] *Ibid.*, p. 103.
[18] Domhoff, *Who Rules America?*, p. 79.

elite universities by members of the power elite has diminished" in the intervening years.

The degree of actual control of university life which this "dominance" entails no doubt greatly varies, and may well in normal circumstances be of a formal kind. But circumstances often tend not to be normal; and whatever that degree of control may be at any time, the influence of lay governors is almost certain to be exercised in conservative directions, and to reinforce in whatever measure is possible the conformist tendencies of the university.[19]

Moreover, in so far as university heads, administrators and teachers are susceptible to other "outside" influences, these influences are also likely to encourage such tendencies. To quote Professor MacIver again, "our colleges and even more our schools are the targets of a tremendous volume of protestations, charges and appeals."[20] He might have added that such protestations, charges and appeals are seldom if ever based on the view that universities are too conservative; it is for their liberalism and their "leniency" towards the dissenters in their midst that university authorities must expect, particularly in times of crisis, to come under attack from the press and a variety of other conservative forces—and not only in the United States.

Fourthly, the growth of corporate enterprise, quite apart from the influence of businessmen, has itself had a profound impact upon the universities. Professor Galbraith has observed that "modern higher education is, of course, extensively accommodated to the needs of the industrial system";[21] and Mr. William Whyte has demonstrated one aspect of this "accommodation" by reference to the fact that, of all the American students who graduated in 1954–5, the largest single group of all (19.4 percent), had been studying business and commerce, *"more than all of the men* in the basic sciences and the liberal arts put together. (And more than all the men in law and medicine and religion. . . .)."[22] Other advanced capitalist countries have still a long way to go before busi-

---

[19] A distinguished American educator wrote in 1930 that "their indirect and, I believe, largely unconscious influence may be and often is, however, considerable . . . In the social and economic realms they create an atmosphere of timidity which is not without effect in critical appointments and in promotion." (A. Flexner, *Universities: American, English, German,* 1930, p. 180, in Beck, *Men Who Control Our Universities,* p. 34). This too is unlikely to have been rendered obsolete with the passage of the years.

[20] MacIver, *Academic Freedom in Our Time,* p. 62.

[21] Galbraith, *The New Industrial State,* 1967, pp. 370–1.

[22] W. H. Whyte, Jr., *The Organisation Man,* 1956, p. 88 (italics in text). See also his chapter 8, "Business Influence on Education."

ness studies assume so prominent a place in their universities. But the proliferation of business administration departments, industrial relations departments, graduate business schools and the like suggests that some of the ground at least is being made up.

There is one characteristic of this type of study which is seldom accorded the attention which it deserves, namely that what it provides for its students is not simply a training in the "techniques of management" and other assorted skills, but also a training in the ideology, values and purposes of capitalist enterprise. Those engaged in such studies, as teachers and students, may conceivably be pursuing the kind of intellectual inquiry which is supposed to be the characteristic of university work: but they are also the servants of a cult, the cult of Mammon.

The university also "accommodates" itself to the demands of business in other ways. "In some cases," Mr. Whyte has also noted, "the business demand has also influenced them in the type of man they favour in the selection of students and the awarding of scholarships. One dean of freshmen told me that in screening applicants from secondary schools he felt it was only common sense to take into account not only what the college wanted but what, four years later, corporations' recruiters would want." [23] In this respect too, other advanced capitalist countries may be lagging behind. But here too there is every reason to believe that universities and their students are becoming increasingly aware of the requirements of business, not only in technical but also in ideological terms.

It is in this perspective that the role of universities as teaching institutions must be set. Both in the appointment of their teachers and in the content of their teaching, universities in the countries of advanced capitalism do retain a very wide degree of formal and actual autonomy—very often an all but absolute autonomy. But that autonomy all the same is exercised within a particular economic, social and political context which deeply affects the universities. This is not to suggest that university authorities and teachers are the bullied victims of outside pressures who are only allowed to exercise their autonomy on condition that they do not do so in ways which offend the powers that be. It may sometimes be so. But it is much more often the case that both university authorities and teachers endorse the context, are *part* of it, and exercise their autonomy in ways which are congruent with that

[23] Whyte, *The Organisation Man*, p. 116.

context, not because they are compelled to do so but because they themselves are moved by conformist modes of thought. Thus, in an address delivered in 1961 to the Alumni Association of Harvard and entitled "The Age of the Scholar," we find Dr. Pusey, then President of Harvard, defending his Economics Faculty and other teachers in the following terms:

Can anyone seriously charge that these men and the others in their departments are subverting the American way of life? And can one seriously charge the same of the university as a whole, taking note of its programme in history, government, public administration and social relations, and its far-reaching effort in business, which is almost completely directed toward making the private enterprise system continue to work effectively and beneficially in a very difficult world? [24]

There are some who might find this kind of grovelling utterly incompatible with the ideals associated with a university. But there is nothing to suggest that its expression did violence to Dr. Pusey's ideas and beliefs, or that he was not presenting an accurate view of the ideology of his teachers.

The point is directly relevant to the appointments policies of the universities. For the tragedy of American universities in the McCarthy era—and after—is not only that many of them were debarred from employing communists and other "subversives"; an equal or even greater tragedy, is that they mostly found little difficulty in endorsing "loyalty" requirements; and that those who were not so debarred used their autonomy and freedom in appointments similarly to exclude such men and often to get rid of them if they had them. It is illuminating in this respect to follow the tortured hesitations of as liberal and humane a university administrator as Dr. Hutchins. On the one hand, "convinced and able Marxists on the faculty may be necessary if the conversation about Marxism is to be anything but hysterical and superficial." On the other, "it may be said that a Marxist cannot think [*sic*] and that therefore he is not eligible for membership in a university community according to my definition of it. *I admit that the presumption is to that effect.*" But then yet again, "I must add that regarding the presumption as irrefutable comes dangerously close to saying that anybody who does not agree with me cannot think." And after seeking to draw a distinction between good members of the Communist Party (i.e. those who, despite

[24] N. M. Pusey, *The Age of the Scholar*, 1963, p. 171. It may be stressed that this address *was* delivered in 1961, and not at the height of the McCarthy era.

the "strong presumption" that there are "few fields in which a member of the Communist Party can think independently," yet may do so) and bad members (i.e. a communist who could not demonstrate his "independence in the field in which he teaches and conducts his research"), Dr. Hutchins goes on to say that:

> Whether I would have had the courage to recommend to our board the appointment of a Marxist, or a bad member of the Communist Party, or a good member whose field was not affected by the Party line *is very dubious indeed*. But *in the most unlikely event* that such persons ever came over my academic horizon, *uniquely qualified* to conduct teaching and research in their chosen fields, I *ought to have had* the courage to say that they should be appointed without regard to their political views or associations.[25]

Such criteria are sufficiently stringent to make it indeed "most unlikely" that Dr. Hutchins would have had an opportunity to test his "courage." At least Dr. Hutchins had qualms. There have always been many others in a similar position to his whose behaviour has suggested that they suffered from fewer inhibitions.

But the matter, to repeat, is not only one of "courage" in the face of external pressure. It is also, and outside the United States much more often, one of quite autonomous suspicion and hostility towards certain forms of intellectual or political unorthodoxy, easily rationalised into a sincerely held belief that such forms of unorthodoxy must, "on academic grounds," at least cast grave doubt on a person's suitability for an academic post, particularly a senior academic post. Most academic economists, for instance, are likely to believe that Marxist economics is nonsense. Their reluctance to see a Marxist economist appointed in their department is therefore not, God forbid, based on anything as vulgar as prejudice, but on the view that no such person could conceivably be a "good economist," not surprisingly since good economists are by definition not Marxists. Such processes of thought, and others akin to them, are a familiar part of the university scene in all advanced capitalist countries. They do not produce anything like an absolute bar on the appointment, and even on the promotion to senior posts, of acutely deviant academics. But they help in the formation

[25] Hutchins, *Freedom, Education and the Fund*, 1956, pp. 158–9 (my italics). Yet Dr. Hutchins also regretfully notes that "nobody would argue that all professors must be members of the Republican Party; but we seem to be approaching the point where they will all be required to be either Republicans or Democrats" (*ibid.*, p. 153).

of a climate in which certain deviant modes of thought and of political commitment find, to put it mildly, very little encouragement indeed—without any external pressure.

The fact that universities are on the whole strongly conformist institutions, most of whose teachers are likely to dwell in their ways of thought within the prevailing spectrum of consensus, cannot but affect the manner in which they fulfil their teaching function.

In the address already quoted, Lord Robbins told the European rectors and vice-chancellors that "we are the universities of free societies; and nothing would be more alien to the spirit of such societies than that we should again become the instruments for the inculcation of particular dogmas or creeds." [26] But, Lord Robbins added, "there is, however, one exception to this rule. There is one creed which the free society cannot repudiate without decreeing its own abdication—the creed of freedom itself." [27]

This is fine but the point needs to be taken further. For the creed of freedom is understood by many people who subscribe to it to include, and even to require, a certain view of the economic, social and political arrangements appropriate to a "free society"; and this, not unnaturally, is very often accompanied by an exceedingly negative approach to all ideas which run counter to that view. In other words, if a man who subscribes to the creed of freedom also believes that free enterprise is an essential part of it, he will find abhorrent all theories of society which posit its abolition. On this view, the creed of freedom holds no guarantee that it will foster among its subscribers the "habit of critical objectivity" which Lord Robbins sees as one of its basic ingredients.[28] After all, it is precisely in the name of freedom that many American universities have engaged, with the utmost sense of rectitude, in the virtual elimination, in terms of appointments, of certain forms of dissent. Mme. Roland's bitter lament, "Liberty, how many crimes have been committed in thy name," might here be rephrased to read, "Freedom, how many orthodoxies have been defended in thy name," and in the name of democracy too.

There are certainly some important senses in which it is true to say that most universities in the countries of advanced capitalism are not "instruments for the inculcation of particular dogmas or

[26] Robbins, *The Universities in the Modern World,* p. 14.
[27] *Ibid.,* p. 14.
[28] *Ibid.,* p. 15.

creeds"; in the sense for instance that neither teachers nor students are generally required to make obeisance to any particular doctrine, party or leader; in the sense that argument is not normally stifled, and is indeed often encouraged; and also because students, in most respectable university institutions, do have access to views and ideas different from and opposed to those offered them by most of their teachers.

These are indeed admirable and precious features of university life. Yet, without in the least belittling them, it has to be noted, in this as in other realms, that the pluralism and diversity which they suggest are not quite as luxuriant as they might at first sight appear to be. For while universities are centres of intellectual, ideological and political diversity, their students are mainly exposed to ideas, concepts, values and attitudes much more designed to foster acceptance of the "conventional wisdom" than acute dissent from it. Many universities may harbour and make available to their students every conceivable current of thought; but everywhere too some currents are very much stronger than others.

Nevertheless, young men and women do often leave their university in a frame of mind more rebellious than when they entered it; and large numbers of students in all capitalist countries (and non-capitalist ones as well for that matter) have dramatically demonstrated that as agencies of socialisation universities have distinct limitations. Students are much more likely to be taught to understand the world in ways calculated to diminish rather than enhance their propensities to change it. Yet the purpose is often defeated by the determination of growing numbers of students to escape the conformist net woven for them by their elders.

This, however, does not affect the point that the pressures towards conformity generated by the university are very strong; and the degree to which universities do remain elite institutions tends to foster among many of those who have gained access to them, not least among students from the working classes, a sense of alienation from the subordinate classes and of empathy with the superior classes, which is not conducive to sustained rebelliousness. Nor certainly is the knowledge that such rebelliousness may well jeopardise the prospect of a career for which, in many cases, particularly in regard to children of the working classes, great personal and parental sacrifices have often been made. Even where such pressures, and many others, are resisted in the course of a university career, the stern expectations of the "outside world" after graduation are such as to induce in many graduates a sense that rebelliousness and nonconformity are expensive luxuries with which it may be prudent to dispense until some future date. But very often, somehow, the future in this sense never comes; instead, erstwhile rebels, safely ensconced in one part or other of the "real world," look back with a mixture of amusement and nostalgia at what they have come to see as youthful aberrations. . . .

Quite clearly, the greatest of all dangers to the capitalist system is that more and more people, particularly in the subordinate classes, should come to think as both possible and desirable an entirely different social order, based upon the social ownership of at least a predominant part of the means of economic activity, and dedicated to the elimination of privilege and unequal power; and that "the masses" should also seek to give expression to this belief in terms of political action.

The main purpose of the process of legitimation which has been described here is precisely to prevent the spread of such consciousness. But that purpose is not only served by the insistence on the virtues of the capitalist *status quo*. It is also served, at least as effectively, by criticism of many aspects of existing economic, social and political arrangements, coupled, however, with the rejection of the socialist alternative to them. That rejection may be based on many different grounds; for instance that the deficiencies of capitalist society, however real, are remediable within its ambit, and without recourse to revolutionary change; or that common ownership affords no guarantee of democracy and equality, which is true, and that it is not necessary to their achievement, which is not; that common ownership is in any case irrelevant to the problems of an "industrial system," which has made the notion of "capitalism" itself obsolete; and so on.

Provided the economic basis of the social order is not called into question, criticism of it, however sharp, can be very useful to it, since it makes for vigorous but safe controversy and debate, and for the advancement of "solutions" to "problems" which obscure and deflect attention from the greatest of all "problems," namely that here is a social order governed by the search for private profit. It is in the formulation of a radicalism without teeth and in the articulation of a critique without dangerous consequences, as well as in terms of straightforward apologetics, that many intellectuals have played an exceedingly "functional" role. And the fact that many of them have played that role with the utmost sincerity and without being conscious of its apologetic import has in no way detracted from its usefulness.

Bibliography

BAILEY, STEPHEN K., RICHARD T. FROST, PAUL E. MARSH, AND ROBERT C. WOOD, *Schoolmen and Politics.* Syracuse, N.Y.: Syracuse University Press, 1962.

BAILEY, STEPHEN K., AND EDITH K. MOSHER, *ESEA: The Office of Education Administers a Law.* Syracuse, N.Y.: Syracuse University Press, 1968.

BALDRIDGE, J. VICTOR, *Academic Governance: Research in Institutional Politics and Decision Making.* Berkeley, Calif.: McCutchan Publishing Corporation, 1971.

BERKE, JOEL S., AND MICHAEL W. KIRST, *Federal Aid to Education: Decision-Making and Allocation.* Lexington, Mass.: D. C. Heath, 1972.

BOWLES, SAMUEL, "Contradictions in Higher Education in the United States," in *The Capitalist System: A Radical Analysis of American Society,* eds. Richard C. Edwards, Michael Reich, and Thomas E. Weisskopf. Englewood Cliffs, N.J.: Prentice-Hall, Inc., 1972.

BRAUN, ROBERT J., *Teachers and Power: The Story of the American Federation of Teachers.* New York: Simon and Schuster, 1972.

BRENTON, MYRON, *What's Happened to Teacher?* New York: Avon Books, 1970.

CALLAHAN, RAYMOND, *Education and the Cult of Efficiency.* Chicago: University of Chicago Press, 1962.

CAMPBELL, ROALD F., LUVERN L. CUNNINGHAM, AND RODERICK S. McPHEE, *The Organization and Control of American Schools.* Columbus, Ohio: Charles E. Merrill Books, Inc., 1965.

COHEN, DAVID, AND MARVIN LAZERSON, "Education and the Corporate Order," *Socialist Revolution,* 8 (March–April, 1972), pp. 47–72.

COLE, STEPHEN, *The Unionization of Teachers: A Case Study of the UFT.* New York: Praeger Publishers, 1969.

COLLINS, RANDALL, "Functional and Conflict Theories of Educational Stratification," *American Sociological Review,* 36 (December, 1971), pp. 1002–19.

CONANT, JAMES B., *The Education of American Teachers.* New York: McGraw-Hill Book Company, 1963.

COUNTS, GEORGE S., *The Social Composition of Boards of Education.* Chicago: University of Chicago Press, 1927.

———, *School and Society in Chicago.* New York: Harcourt, Brace, 1928.

CRAIN, ROBERT L., *The Politics of School Desegregation.* Chicago: Aldine Publishing Company, 1968.

CRAIN, ROBERT L., AND JAMES J. VANECKO, "Elite Influence in School Desegregation," in *City Politics and Public Policy,* ed. James Q. Wilson. New York: John Wiley & Sons, 1968.

CRONIN, JOSEPH M., *The Control of Urban Schools.* Riverside, N.J.: The Free Press, 1973.

CURTI, MERLE, *The Social Ideas of American Educators.* Totowa, N.J.: Littlefield, Adams & Co., 1959 (originally published in 1935).

FANTINI, MARIO, MARILYN GITTELL, AND RICHARD MAGAT, *Community Control and the Urban School.* New York: Praeger Publishers, 1970.

GITTELL, MARILYN, *Participants and Patricipation: A Study of School Policy in New York City.* New York: Praeger Publishers, 1967.

GITTELL, MARILYN, AND ALAN G. HEVESI, eds., *The Politics of Urban Education.* New York: Praeger Publishers, 1969.

GITTELL, MARILYN, AND T. EDWARD HOLLANDER, *Six Urban School Districts: A Comparative Study of Institutional Response.* New York: Praeger Publishers, 1968.

GREER, COLIN, *The Great School Legend: A Revisionist Interpretation of American Education.* New York: Basic Books, 1972.

GROSS, NEAL, *Who Runs Our Schools?* New York: John Wiley & Sons, 1958.

HARTNETT, RODNEY T., *College and University Trustees: Their Backgrounds, Roles and Educational Attitudes.* Princeton, N.J.: Educational Testing Service, 1969.

HUNTER, FLOYD, *Community Power Structure: A Study of Decision Makers.* Chapel Hill, N.C.: University of North Carolina Press, 1953.

IANNACCONE, LAURENCE, *Politics in Education.* New York: Center for Applied Research in Education, 1967.

JENCKS, CHRISTOPHER, AND DAVID RIESMAN, *The Academic Revolution.* Garden City, N.Y.: Doubleday & Company, 1968.

KARIER, CLARENCE J., PAUL VIOLAS, AND JOEL SPRING, *Roots of Crisis: American Education in the Twentieth Century.* Chicago: Rand McNally, 1973.

KATZ, MICHAEL, *The Irony of Early School Reform: Educational Innovation in Mid-Nineteenth Century Massachusetts.* Cambridge, Mass.: Harvard University Press, 1968.

———, *Class, Bureaucracy, and Schools: The Illusion of Educational Change in America.* New York: Praeger Publishers, 1971.

KIMBROUGH, RALPH B., *Political Power and Educational Decision-Making.* Chicago: Rand McNally, 1964.

KIRST, MICHAEL W., ed., *The Politics of Education at the Local, State and Federal Levels.* Berkeley, Calif.: McCutchan Publishing Corporation, 1970.

——, ed., *State, School, and Politics: Research Directions.* Lexington, Mass.: D. C. Heath, 1972.

KOERNER, JAMES D., *The Miseducation of American Teachers.* Baltimore: Penguin Books, Inc., 1963.

——, *Who Controls American Education?* Boston: Beacon Press, 1968.

LANOUE, GEORGE R., AND BRUCE L. R. SMITH, *Politics of School Decentralization.* Lexington, Mass.: D. C. Heath, 1972.

LAUTER, PAUL, AND ARCHIBALD W. ALEXANDER, "ACE: Defender of the Educational Faith," *The Antioch Review,* 29 (Fall, 1969), pp. 287–303.

LAZERSON, MARVIN, *Origins of the Urban School: Public Education in Massachusetts, 1870–1915.* Cambridge, Mass.: Harvard University Press, 1971.

——, "Revisionism and American Educational History," *Harvard Educational Review,* 43 (May, 1973), pp. 269–283.

LEE, EUGENE C., AND FRANK M. BOWEN, *The Multicampus University: A Study of Academic Governance.* New York: McGraw-Hill Book Company, 1971.

LEVIN, HENRY M., ed., *Community Control of Schools.* New York: Simon and Schuster, 1972.

MARTIN, ROSCOE, *Government and the Suburban School.* Syracuse, N.Y.: Syracuse University Press, 1962.

MASSIALAS, BYRON G., *Education and the Political System.* Reading, Mass.: Addison-Wesley Publishing Company, 1969.

MASTERS, NICHOLAS A., ROBERT H. SALISBURY, AND THOMAS H. ELIOT, *State Politics and the Public Schools.* New York: Alfred A. Knopf, 1964.

MAYER, MARTIN, *The Teachers Strike: New York, 1968.* New York: Harper and Row, 1968.

MERANTO, PHILIP, *The Politics of Federal Aid to Education in 1965: A Study in Political Innovation.* Syracuse, N.Y.: Syracuse University Press, 1967.

MILES, MICHAEL W., *The Radical Probe: The Logic of Student Rebellion.* New York: Atheneum, 1971.

POIS, JOSEPH, *The School Board Crisis: A Chicago Case Study.* Chicago: Educational Methods, 1964.

RIDGEWAY, JAMES, *The Closed Corporation: American Universities in Crisis.* New York: Ballantine Books, 1968.

ROGERS, DAVID, *110 Livingston Street: Politics and Bureaucracy in the New York City School System.* New York: Random House, 1968.

ROSENTHAL, ALAN, ed., *Governing Education: A Reader on Politics, Power, and Public School Policy.* Garden City, N.Y.: Doubleday & Company, 1969.

——, *Pedagogues and Power: Teacher Groups in School Politics.* Syracuse, N.Y.: Syracuse University Press, 1969.

RUBIN, LILLIAN B., *Busing and Backlash: White against White in an Urban School District*. Berkeley, Calif.: University of California Press, 1972.

SAYRE, WALLACE S., AND HERBERT KAUFMAN, *Governing New York City: Politics in the Metropolis*. New York: Russell Sage Foundation, 1960.

SCHRAG, PETER, *Village School Downtown*. Boston: Beacon Press, 1967.

SCHUDSON, MICHAEL S., "Organizing the 'Meritocracy': A History of the College Entrance Examination Board," *Harvard Educational Review*, 42 (February, 1972), pp. 34–69.

SEXTON, PATRICIA C., *The American School: A Sociological Analysis*. Englewood Cliffs, N.J.: Prentice-Hall, Inc., 1967.

SPRING, JOEL H., *Education and the Rise of the Corporate State*. Boston: Beacon Press, 1972.

USDAN, MICHAEL V., *The Political Power of Education in New York State*. New York: The Institute of Administrative Research, Teachers College, Columbia University, 1963.

VEBLEN, THORSTEIN, *The Higher Learning in America: A Memorandum on the Conduct of Universities by Business Men*. New York: Hill and Wang, 1957 (originally published in 1918).

VIDICH, ARTHUR J., AND JOSEPH BENSMAN, *Small Town in Mass Society*. Princeton, N.J.: Princeton University Press, 1958.

WASSERMAN, MIRIAM, *The School Fix, NYC, USA*. New York: Outerbridge and Dienstfrey, 1970.

WHITE, ALPHEUS L., *Local School Boards: Organizations and Practices*. Washington, D.C.: Government Printing Office, 1962.

WIRT, FREDERICK M., AND MICHAEL W. KIRST, *The Political Web of American Schools*. Boston: Little, Brown and Company, 1972.

WOLFE, ALAN, "Reform Without Reform: The Carnegie Commission on Higher Education," *Social Policy*, 2 (May, June, 1971), pp. 18–27.